LOVE YOUR ENEMIES
...AND OTHER NEIGHBOURS

WORKSHOPS FOR PEACE

MEDITATIONS

◆ WORSHIP ◆

ART ◆ MUSIC

BOB HAVERLUCK

THE UNITED CHURCH PUBLISHING HOUSE

Copyright © 1992 The United Church Publishing House

All rights reserved. No part of this book may be reproduced, stored in a retrieval system, or transmitted, in any form or by any means, electronic, mechanical, photocopying, recording, or otherwise, without the written permission of The United Church Publishing House.

An exception is made to the above restriction with respect to items in the section "Musings." Permission is granted to photocopy excerpts for worship and meditation purposes, one time use only, not to be sold.

Unless otherwise stated, all biblical quotations and references are from *The New Jerusalem Bible*.

Canadian Cataloguing in Publication Data

Haverluck, Bob, 1945-

Love your enemies – and other neighbours
Includes bibliographical references.

ISBN 0-919000-65-7

1. Conflct management – Religious aspects – Christianity.
2. Interpersonal relations – Religious aspects - Christianity. 3. Peace – Religious aspects - Christianity. I. Title.

BT736.4.H38 1991 248.4 C91-095237-X

The United Church Publishing House
85 St. Clair Avenue East
Toronto, Ont.
M4T 1M8

Publisher: R.L. Naylor
Editor-in-Chief: Peter Gordon White
Editorial Assistant: Elizabeth Phinney
Book Design & Production: David Beyer,
  Department of Graphics & Print
Printed in Canada by: Gagné Printing Ltd.

5 4 3 2 1 92 93 94 95

*This work, and play, is dedicated to Gerry
and to all my friends and enemies
who helped make it possible.*

CONTENTS

viii	Preface
x	A Word to My Reader
xi	About the "Musings"
xii	Using This Book for Worship and Meditation
xii	Hints for the Animator
1	**Workshop One** Hope is where the heart is: unfurling images of hope.
16	**Workshop Two** Crying over spilled milk: rising up against injustice, violence, and the disintegration of creation.
28	**Workshop Three** "Oh ya, but what about the Samaritans, Russians, Iraqis?": mixed messages in the biblical stories about war and peace.
39	**Workshop Four** "Love them? I'd kiss a pig first!": imagining the enemy.
50	**Workshop Five** Turn the cheek; turn the tables; turn direction: loving the powerful by opposition.
65	**Workshop Six** "Don't make me laugh!": satire as necessary medicine.
80	**Workshop Seven** No more bucks for the Bang: the economic appeals of militarism.
93	**Workshop Eight** "See my finger, see my thumb, see my missile – you'd better run!": the dogma of deterrence.
110	**Workshop Nine** The farce of force: discovering our security in "Common Security."
130	**Workshop Ten** "Where two or three are gathered . . . ": going from here.
142	Selected Bibliography
143	Acknowledgements

PREFACE

In Prague's jazz clubs, poetry and politics mix with blues laments. Here the "too few" encourage one another to dream of a peaceable country and a peaceable world. Here persistent acts of non-violent resistance are reported and rehearsed. It is 1968. It is 1977. It is 1989. It often seems a waste of time, and yet . . .

In a Protestant church in East Berlin, several old and young gather. Again they read of a Christ who is a cunning wind up the trousers of arrogance and power and, again, are blown into the streets to join small protests for less militarism and more democracy. It is 1968. It is 1977. It is 1989. It often seems a waste of time, and yet . . .

In a university coffee shop in Moscow, poets, students, and left-wing "politicos" unfold visions: fear will be a memory and public debates amidst bread and wine be more than mere dreaming. It is 1968. It is 1977. It is 1989. It often seems a waste of time, and yet . . .

In a United Church basement, a handful gather with a Bible in one hand and a newspaper in the other. They brood over Canada's complicity in Vietnam, in Pinochet's Chile, in America's Gulf War, and other cruelties as unbending as an iron curtain or a wall in Berlin. These few worship and study and join with others outside this place, others who disturb the false peace of an order without enough mercy, law without justice. It is 1968. It is 1977. It is 1992. It often seems to make little difference, and yet . . .

These representative groups of peacemakers did not bring about the dismantling of the iron curtain by themselves, alone. They did dream and rehearse it, however. They persisted in working when voices without and within snorted that it was "a waste of time." The persistence of these myriad clusters of peacemakers is not the news that is broadcast in our country, however. Is it because their example is as troubling to the capitalist marketplace, and its attendant military muscle, as it was to the machinations of the rulers behind the supposedly eternal iron curtain?

In the Gospel of Luke, Jesus compares his contemporaries to two groups of children shouting at one another. The two groups seem to be shouting very different things. One group says: "We played the pipes for you, and you wouldn't dance," and the other: "We sang dirges, and you wouldn't cry" (Luke 7:32). Yet the two groups are in agreement. As they shout back and forth in the marketplace, they are tacitly agreeing not to move; just to sit. In this way, the business of buying and selling is undisturbed. The activity of the marketplace, with its hidden and not so hidden violence, is uninterrupted. There is no movement sparked by dance and/or dirge, because neither the merriment nor the mourning are played out.

In genuine dance (i.e. not merely mechanical), we move through and beyond the steps or laws of the dance. Similarly when we cry, we come into conflict with the hard "given" of things; the limits of our reality. Both dancing and crying, joy and sorrow, offer a visceral way of questioning the expected order, but only if we dance and cry from the heart.

These workshops are exhortations to dance and to weep, in the face of a marketplace that endorses violence. Our marketplace is in the church, as well as outside it, just as it was inside and outside the temple grounds in Jesus' time. The market is never so surely in the church as when the church pretends that it isn't. Now, as in Jesus' time, the military dimension of the market is questioned. We question its laws with our God-induced sense of what truly makes for joy and for sorrow. The workshops begin with a sense of joyful grace, and move on to explore the refusals of grace that precipitate so much sorrow. As the workshops proceed, we move, like children at serious play, between the extremes of dance and dirge.

Why do we need peacemaking workshops, worship, or meditation? This question may be asked from very different positions: (1) trust in American military technology, used in Iraq and ready for any other trouble-spot; (2) belief in a God who is not interested in the suffering, degradation, and death that violence entails; (3) despair and despondency that are raised by the deadly "facts" of reality. People who hold these positions are unmoved by the memory and the hope of the resurrection. The material in this book addresses these and other positions common in a society that refuses to believe in peace.

The workshops move us toward an increasingly comprehensible approach to peacemaking. The hands, no less than the heart and head, are given attention. Each area has its needs. Each one wants, and gets, its turn. For if the aim of peacemaking is not only to begin but to persist, then head, heart, and hands must work together. When each of these is friend and ally to the others, we are better prepared for peacemaking over the long haul.

I express my gratitude to those who helped spark and test the ideas in this resource: Dr. Stan McKay Jr. and the Dr. Jessie Saulteaux Resource Centre; the Prairie Christian Training Centre; Regents Park United Church; Shoal Lake-Decker pastoral charge; the Brandon United Nations Youth Seminar; and friends Gerry, Paul, Mom, Dad, Ben, Eleanor, Dudley, Ian, Janet, Ethel, Bob, Shari, Ed, Johanna, Lorraine . . . to name but some who offered support and encouragement. Also, grants from the United Church "Peace Fund" and the

Canada Council "Explorations Program" have helped this work come about. Thanks also for ongoing encouragement from the magazines and journals that continue to use my drawings in spite of receiving certain letters, and in spite of not receiving others. I am grateful to all.

A WORD TO MY READER

This is my invitation to you to discern in conflict an opportunity to turn enemies into friends; to learn how we can be turned from other people's enemies into their friends. The process is both personal and political, both local and international in scope. The workshops outlined here are meant for workshop participants and leaders. They are also intended as an invitation to the general reader who wishes to join in the exercises, meditations, and prayers and begin the peace process personally.

The strategy of this book is to work with more than just our heads, our hearts, or our hands. Involved here are all these things: our mind's understanding, our heart's fears and hopes, and our local response to what is ultimately a global problem. The fact that we cannot do everything doesn't mean that there is nothing we can do. Yet that hopeless conclusion is often drawn. Consequently, the point of these workshops is to encourage us to think more clearly about these matters; to laugh, cry, and sigh about them and to uncover openings where we can dig in, and work toward peace.

All this is done within the embrace of our faith. More precisely, it is accomplished within God's embrace and God's faithfulness. It is my hope that working and playing through the stories, prayers, and songs will help turn us toward God's creation and teach us to re-create in the spirit of mercy.

Bob Haverluck

ABOUT THE "MUSINGS"

t the end of each workshop is a collection of musings, consisting of quotations, cartoons, and poetry. Musings are intended to unfold themes from the last workshop, either by pushing deeper into the topic, or by offering a different angle for reflection. Musings are meant as vehicles for meditation between workshops. In this way our workshop discoveries and insights are not only remembered but brooded over between meetings and further developed.

I suggest that this be done in three ways: (1) by encouraging participants to take time each week to reflect on the material on their own; (2) by having each participant keep a journal or diary of their thoughts, questions, and feelings on these matters; and (3) by talking on the phone or in person with a regular conversation-partner throughout the workshop period. A weekly conversation will allow participants to share and explore insights and confusions. Both meditation on and conversation about one's thoughts are important elements in the life of any peace and justice worker. Like many workshop activities, the reading-meditations and the conversations are rehearsals for what may become ordinary, everyday behaviour.

Some people may not know how to muse or meditate. One suggestion is "simply begin." Reading and re-reading the material two, three, or four times can be helpful. We should not be surprised to find that some things do not make complete sense on first or even second reading. The ideas suggested may, like pomegranates, be hard to peel, but savouring their taste makes it worthwhile. In short, be prepared to be patient in the face of our own lack of understanding. It is also helpful to take what we understand and say it in our own words, perhaps aloud to the dog. Or write it down. Or a combination of the two. (If the dog can read, that will also be helpful.) Take the material from this process into periods of quiet; explicitly ask for God's help in understanding it, and responding to it. That is the crux of this workshop meditation. When it comes to sharing with our conversation partner we may well have something to offer and may well be more receptive to receiving and exploring together.

USING THIS BOOK FOR WORSHIP AND MEDITATION

Apart from the extensive "worship" materials and the "musings" (with their collected readings and cartoons), many workshop exercises could be used for meditation or worship. For example, the heart of workshop 3, which focuses on contradictory scriptural messages about the treatment of enemies, could be recast for the sermon period of worship. Relevant readings could be used and discussed if groups were limited to three or four. The worship leader might gather a sampling of the group's questions and conclusions to be explored in greater depth if refreshments were served following the worship.

To the individual reader of my book, I suggest you perform the workshop exercises in your imagination. You will then find that writing a journal will help give shape to the emotions and ideas that arise in this form of meditation.

HINTS FOR THE ANIMATOR

The animator plays a crucial role in helping to establish a safe and welcoming space and time. The role requires that the animator take the time to prepare carefully for each workshop. As experienced hands know, it is organization and preparation that create a relaxed animator: one who is attentive to the group's dynamic and able to nurture a playful yet serious spirit. The drawing of an animator on the following page may say it all, but let me share these practical hints with you.

Participants should enter a workspace that makes them feel expected and prepared for. There are a number of things you can do beforehand that will create that atmosphere: hang posters or prints that touch some of our themes; unstack chairs and arrange in a close circle so that everyone feels a degree of intimacy; play music that sets the tone of the workshop and allows for quiet conversation.

The space you choose should be large enough to allow for the kind of movement that workshops sometimes involve. Nearby space for small group work will be handy from time to time.

Pre-reading all the workshops will give you a sense of their necessary direction and flow. A more detailed reading of at least two workshops ahead will help you gather resource materials. It will also help you make the necessary announcements about the upcoming workshop.

Before leading each workshop, the animator will want to read and walk through the upcoming workshop step-by-step in his or her imagination. This will help the animator feel more confident and relaxed in the task.

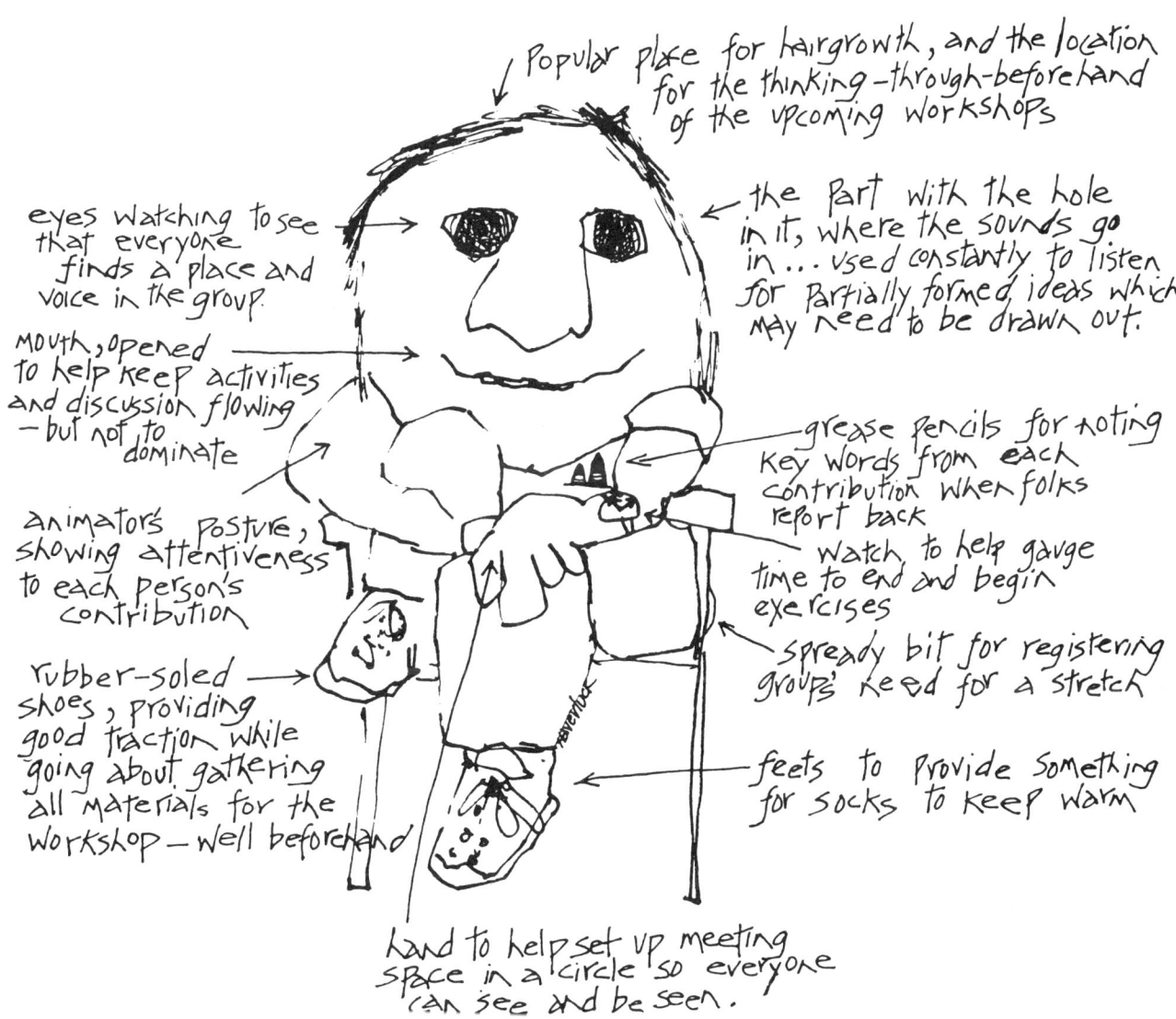

Hints for the Animator

To vary the voices of those who contribute, to exercises or worship, pre-plan and give other readers time to prepare. Involving several voices helps give folks a greater sense of contribution and participation, and the variety is pleasing to the ear.

The workshops are designed with groups of about eight people in mind. Larger groups mean breaking into small groups or pairs, and individuals reporting to the main group periodically. Large groups will likely require workshop timing adjustments.

A word about the size of working groups vis-a-vis particular workshop exercises may be helpful. Before large or total group discussion, encourage individuals to spend a little time alone. Solitude allows less verbally skilled people to organize their thoughts and feelings before engaging others.

Pairing is also used extensively. It allows two people the opportunity for discussion in a limited time period. When dealing with issues that cause anxiety and uncertainty, pairing allows for greater intimacy, if that is desired. It reminds the quick and determined talkers of their responsibility to listen. Slow and tentative talkers often find pairings less intimidating.

Small groupings that have been preceded by individual and paired reflection have a habit of being much more participatory and productive. If there is a high trust level in your group, you may wish to use more small group discussion and fewer pairings. However, if people are shy or untrusting, larger group work will have to be slowly introduced because our subject matter involves a high degree of self-disclosure.

When receiving information in the total group be sure to list on the flip chart a key word or phrase from each contributor. This helps the participants see that you are listening to and hearing them. If you're unclear about their position, ask for clarification so that you avoid "putting words in their mouths."

During a session the animator and the group may decide that altering the proposed workshop design is desirable. You must gauge when it is important to talk topics through and when they can simply be suggested for reflection and discussed later. This method presupposes that we can live with difference and without agreement on every aspect of an issue.

The animator may need to find her or his own way of presenting the workshops. You will notice that the material is printed with two audiences in mind: the animator and the participant. The italicized material is composed as if it is spoken directly to workshop participants. You will decide whether or not you want to assume this voice.

Hints for the Animator

Other material is in the form of directions for the animator. In either case you will need to adjust the material to suit your own personality. Knowing your group and your own way of relating will help you decide how you will use this material, and what you will use of it. You may decide to alter the material and the order as well.

I have organized the workshops to begin with the gospel, for it is the gospel that brings us together in the first place. We begin there. We move on to the more explicitly political content. We discover ways in which faith imperatives can shape actions and structures in the wider world.

These workshops are designed to exercise (and exorcise) the heart, the head, and the hands. Our assumption is that to feel confident as peace workers, we must be as comfortable as possible working within all of these dimensions. Issues surrounding the creation of war and the creation of peace are explored in their theological context, political context, and in their social action context. Worship remains a constant feature of all the workshops.

Each person, because of character and context, may emphasize a different dimension. Nevertheless, workshop time offers an opportunity to explore and to develop confidence in underdeveloped aspects of the issue of peacemaking. It is essentially a playtime, a safe space and time to try on different perspectives and approaches. It gives different individuals a chance to plan and rehearse new directions.

To close on a practical note, the music for worship and the cartoon clusters referred to in the workshops follow the Worship section of each workshop.

WORKSHOP 1

Hope is where the heart is: unfurling images of hope.

Scripture helps us to glimpse visions of peace. Unlike "political realism," biblical visions propose guidelines and alternative actions to establish peace. Peace is the absence of war, but not *merely* the absence of war; similarly, war is more than simply a military matter. War concerns injustice, death, disease, madness, and so on.

In biblical terms, peace means security for all and not only for the wealthy and the powerful. Peace is a restoration of justice. It is a process of healing the earth and its inhabitants and their relations – human, animal, and plant: in other words, the relation between God and all creation.

When Christ restored broken hearts, fed the hungry, and healed the sick, he enlivened worn out images of peace among the people. In so doing, Christ stirred promising visions and equipped followers for a better life in an uneasy present and future. This workshop helps us apply biblical visions of peace for all creation to our own time and place.

Objectives:
- To build feelings of comfort and trust in the group.
- To gain a sense of the variety of viewpoints that people bring to the group.
- To explore the content of biblical visions of peace through imagery and visualization.
- To consider how biblical imagery compares with contemporary imagery.

PART A

(15 min.)

Activity 1
After everyone is seated in a circle, put participants at ease by introducing them to the process which will follow. It could go something like this:

Beginning work together as a group often feels a little awkward. It helps to know the name and something about each person. There are many silly games used to help groups through this stage. Our method is not all that silly. It is, perhaps, a little strange, and it requires your imagination to help it work.

Begin by closing your eyes. Now, imagine yourself as a peacemaker in this violent world. If you were to have a companion, a wise aunt or uncle like Mary Magdalene or Martin Luther King Jr., whom would you choose to talk with regularly? Choose someone from historical or contemporary times.

We'll now move around the circle in this way. First one person gives his or her name and companion. Example: "My name is Bob and my uncle is St. Francis." Everyone in the group then repeats together, "Bob and St. Francis." The next person, before giving his or her name and companion, which everyone repeats, gives the name and companion of everyone who went before themselves: "Bob and St. Francis, Ethel and Dorothy Day," and so on. This continues until we've worked all the way 'round the circle.

After this exercise most people will know one another's name. It never fails! They will have something to associate with each person and will begin to feel accepted as part of the group, having heard their name and that of their valued companion spoken at least once (and perhaps fifteen times by everyone). If you have more than fifteen, you should divide into groups of eight or so.

(20 min.)

Activity 2
Most people are familiar with a "bingo dance." When the caller hollers "Bingo!" everyone changes partners. What follows is a series of "bingo conversations."

Participants are asked to join with one other person whom they do not know well, and to share something about their chosen spiritual companion and to tell why they were chosen. Tell everyone that after a few minutes you will ring a little bell, or say "Bingo," or whatever, and have them choose another partner to visit with. It's helpful to acknowledge that it will take a little time before some conversations are completed. Remind people that there will be more opportunities for them to get to know one another.

After two such conversations of four or five minutes in length, you might ask a new question that would lead into two more short conversations. You might ask a question such as, "Who is a person you would never want counsel from, and why?"

(30 min.)

Activity 3
The following cartoon exercise will allow people to become more familiar with one another in a non-threatening fashion.

Individuals are asked to look at the cluster of cartoons that follow at the end of the workshop. They are then asked to go through and choose one cartoon they like and one cartoon they *don't like*. (Our working assumption here is that we can learn an immense amount if we take as much care to understand what troubles us as what pleases us.)

When ready, people can share their cartoon "finds" in pairs. They should be asked to share what they chose and, if they can, why. The objective is not to convince the other of the rightness or the wrongness of the choice. It is to help each person understand what led the other person to be pleased or troubled by what they saw.

To close off this exercise, invite various people to tell the whole group what they chose. Avoid being drawn off into a group discussion. Simply let folks catch a sense of what they enjoy or do not enjoy, in common.

PART B

(45 min.)

Activity 1

Before the group is asked to explore biblical images of peace, a short introduction to the uniqueness of the biblical vision will prove useful. Perhaps something along these lines could be used.

Visions of a world at peace are found at the beginning and end of scripture. The first vision of humankind and all the creatures living in concord is in a garden. In the final vision, the central image is a garden-city. Between the first and the last garden of peace are many stories about coming to terms with the harsh realities of the city. The builder of the first city, Cain, was also the first murderer. The last city, the holy city, is metaphorically built by Christ, the murder victim of its keepers.

There is a pattern for us to keep in mind. One scriptural tradition sees the "wild" creature, representative of the harsh realities of the countryside, as excluded from God's peaceable commonwealth. Another, more extensive tradition insists that there is no real peace without all of nature partaking of it, including the healed city. In biblical imagery, wild things – from weeds to bears to wild water – sometimes represent more than nature. They may represent what is "evil" or "dirty" in the racial or social realm. For example, Israel's enemies may be symbolized by bears, thorns, or a threatening sea. In any case, recurring visions of peacefulness replace arrogance and narrow-mindedness with understanding and inclusiveness.

A second key scriptural pattern to keep in mind is the persistent concept of peace as more than the mere end of war. The ancient Roman word for peace, "pax," and the Greek "eirene," mean simply a period of truce, a pause in hostilities, a comma in an endless sentence of violence, intimidation, and war. In the Bible, peace means the end of violent conflict. However, biblical peace also entails making whole what has been broken . . . restoring relationships between people, between people and God, between nature and humankind, and so on. Peace signifies justice and mercy for all the elements of creation, including both the furry and the non-furry.

Finally, a word about the common context of scriptural passages that envision peace. They often arise in communities facing crises. Is this surprising? If all is well, who needs hopeful visions? Yet, who dares look at what is not well without visions of hope? Without visions of peace, which of us can long ponder or work amidst the crises facing us? For this reason, the workshop series begins with the end: with the God blessed end-vision we seek to live for and work toward. This vision of peace helps sustain our lives in the meantime.

Now for more playful work. What follows is a sampling of scriptural passages that envision something of God's kingdom or commonwealth of peace: Isaiah 9:1-6, 11:1-12; Hosea 2:20-25; Ezekiel 34:23-31; Mark 4:30-32; Colossians 1:15-20.

Read these passages over two or three times. Close your Bible. Gather up some materials for a collage, and then find a quiet corner to work in. There are paper, crayons, and magazines with which you can make a collage or draw. Feel free to use cut-out pictures or picture bits, words, phrases, or your own drawing or writing. The objective of this exercise is not to create a work of art. It's more like a big doodle. The objective is for each of us to ponder and play with our own image of what God's healed or mended creation, God's peaceable commonwealth, might be like. Be messy. Take your time. Try different things. Sometimes creating can be a kind of listening.

(45 min.)

Activity 2

After forty-five minutes or so, people are asked to exchange their creation with one other person. Some questions to encourage discussion might include:

- *Why did you choose the images and phrases you did?*
- *What did you decide to leave out or to add, and why?*
- *How do you feel about the vision that emerged from your work?*

Within the whole group, each person is invited to share one image or phrase from his or her drawing or collage and to tell why they included it in their piece. Allow questions of clarification, but discourage discussion at this point. There will be time in future weeks to explore one another's positions. This process is simply to give participants an early sense of other folks' ways of seeing. This stage is designed to help people feel the excitement of envisioning good possibilities without needing, at this point, to think too hard about defending them or getting stuck on details.

(5 min.)

Activity 3

Before closing worship, give folks some sense of the workshops that are to follow. People may have questions to ask. An introduction to the "Musings" (see page xi), used between workshops, should be given here.

PART C

(20 min.)

Worship

1. Words of Gathering:

*Come vision seekers
eager for God's peaceable commonwealth.
Be in the mystery,
the mercy and strength
of the Creator's creating
and making new.*

2. Let us join in a dialogue of praise taken from a children's peace liturgy.

Leader: Who dances in the dancers' dance and dances on the metal strings when the singers sing?

People: *God dances, dances in everybody's eyes that dream of water running in the hard and stony.*

Leader: Who laughs when dogs are talking and ducks walking with wet feet safely down our city streets?

People: *God laughs in the wind and in the trees waving as water running in the hard and stony.*

Leader: Who sings, when the stars come out, a song for the light of day, for the dark of night?

People: *God sings the songs we hear when the moon shines on water running in the hard and stony.*

Leader: Who cries when poor children cry at the bang and boom blast of bombs?

People: *God cries tears big and bitter as the sea as water running in the hard and stony.*

Leader: Who holds the brown sparrow swaying on the wire; Who holds us, small and big, even when we're tired?

People: *God holds the world, even when it's hard, even when it's hard and stony, God holds the world with a spirit sweet, sweet as water and honey.*

Leader and People: So hurray, hurray, a million, million cheers and praise to God who gives us breath and bread and this day, to God who makes the green grass and the yellow sun, to God who makes the growling bear and the honey bee, the maker and the mender of you and me – the maker and the mender of everyone. Amen.

Workshop 1

3. In a moment, we shall have a prayer of gratitude, regret, and plea. To help us prepare, "Maggie" is going to take a strong thread and tie it around us until we are all joined. As she does this, and each of us offers a hand or body for her to encircle, we shall prepare for prayer. I ask you to imagine this thread as not only attaching us one to another, but as extending to the water, the animals, the air, the people of every place and land. Consider how this is a matter of thanksgiving, confession, and wanting good for others, feathered and non-feathered.

One end of the thread could be attached to the doorknob and the other end to a Bible or cross or candle at the centre of your worship space. If the thread is merely wrapped around people and not literally tied, the thread can be easily detached at the worship's conclusion. Save the thread and place it among the symbols used in upcoming worship times.

(This thread could be imaginatively incorporated into other workshops and used in place of suggested exercises or meditation elements. For example, it could be cut and each person given a piece for meditation whereby the thread becomes a metaphor for severed or broken relationships. It could be used as part of warm-up exercises at the beginning of a future workshop. Folks could be entangled and encouraged to discuss their situation as curse and blessing and so on. You could probably do ten weeks of workshops using a piece of thread in fifty different ways.)

4. What follows is sometimes called a "bidding" prayer. It is a prayer that "Paul" will lead us into, and during the prayer we will be invited to contribute to the prayer by voicing our reaction or by offering it in silence. Following this, Paul will conclude the prayer.

Let us pray:

O Holy Maker and Mender
    Blessed be your name above every name
    on the stock exchange or on the news.
    Blessed be you, Holy Weaver of creation's fine
    and rough threads
    entwining rivers and trees, earth to sky
    me to we, we to them, without end . . .
    except in You, Creator of new beginnings.
    Hear our prayers, O God, as we speak aloud to you,
    or silently in our hearts,
    of gratitude, sorrow, and hope and. . . .
    (period of silence)

*Hear our prayers, O God, and enlarge our sense
of your creation and re-creation.
Enlarge our sense of your presence
in the stuff of the everyday and the holy days
and the bad days.
In Christ's name, we ask it. Amen.*

5. Let us read in unison a fifteenth-century Irish hymn composed by St. Patrick and often called "St. Patrick's Breastplate."

*I bind unto myself today
the strong name of the Trinity,
by invocation of the same,
the three in one, and one in three.*

*I bind this day to me for ever,
by power of faith, Christ's incarnation,
his baptism in Jordan river,
his death on cross for my salvation,
his bursting from the spiced tomb,
his riding up the heavenly way,
his coming at the day of doom,
I bind unto myself today.*

*I bind unto myself today
the virtues of the star-lit heaven,
the glorious sun's life-giving ray,
the whiteness of the moon at even,
the flashing of the lightning free,
the whirling wind's tempestuous shocks,
the stable earth, the deep salt sea
around the old eternal rocks.*

*I bind unto myself today
the power of God to hold and lead,
his eye to watch, his might to stay,
his ear to hearken to my need,
the wisdom of my God to teach,
his hand to guide, his shield to ward,
the word of God to give me speech,
his heavenly host to be my guard.*

*Christ be with me, Christ within me,
Christ behind me, Christ before me,
Christ beside me, Christ to win me,
Christ to comfort and restore me.*

*Christ beneath me, Christ above me,
Christ in quiet, Christ in danger,
Christ in hearts of all that love me,
Christ in mouth of friend and stranger.*

*I bind unto myself the name,
the strong name of the Trinity,
by invocation of the same,
the three in one, and one in three,
of whom all nature hath creation,
eternal Father, Spirit, Word.
Praise to the Lord of my salvation;
salvation is of Christ the Lord.*

6. Benediction:

*Go now in the good company of God the Father,
who Mothers us,
Christ the Brother and Lord,
and our Sister, the Holy Spirit. Amen.*

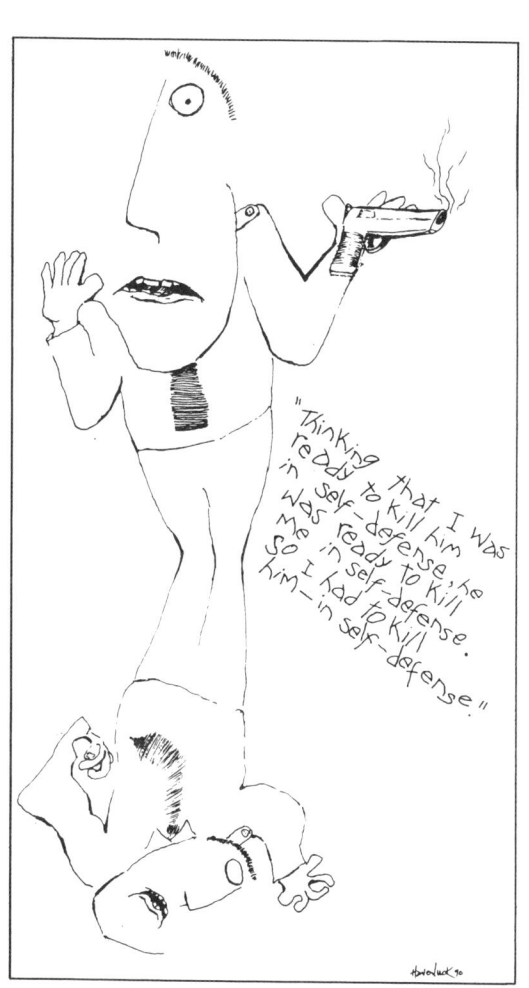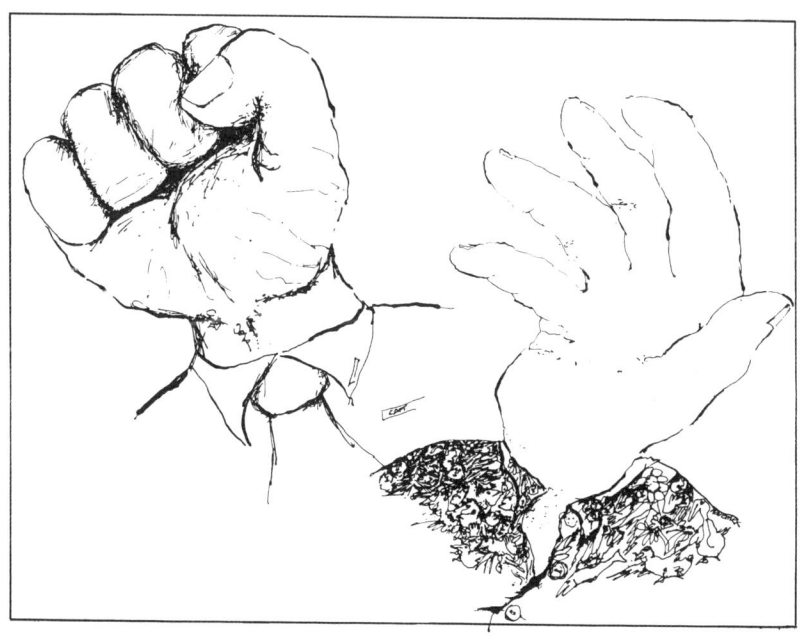

FOR THE INTERVIEW, WE WANT YOU TO WEAR ONE OF THESE

A man picking berries from a berry bush is a symbol of man's relationship to nature. The berry bush or nature has what man wants. He grabs the bush and bends it so he can get at it more easily. He then simply takes the berries as his reward. Incidentally... it's hardly worth mentioning... the recoil power of a ten foot berry bush is 1300 pounds.

Love Your Enemies

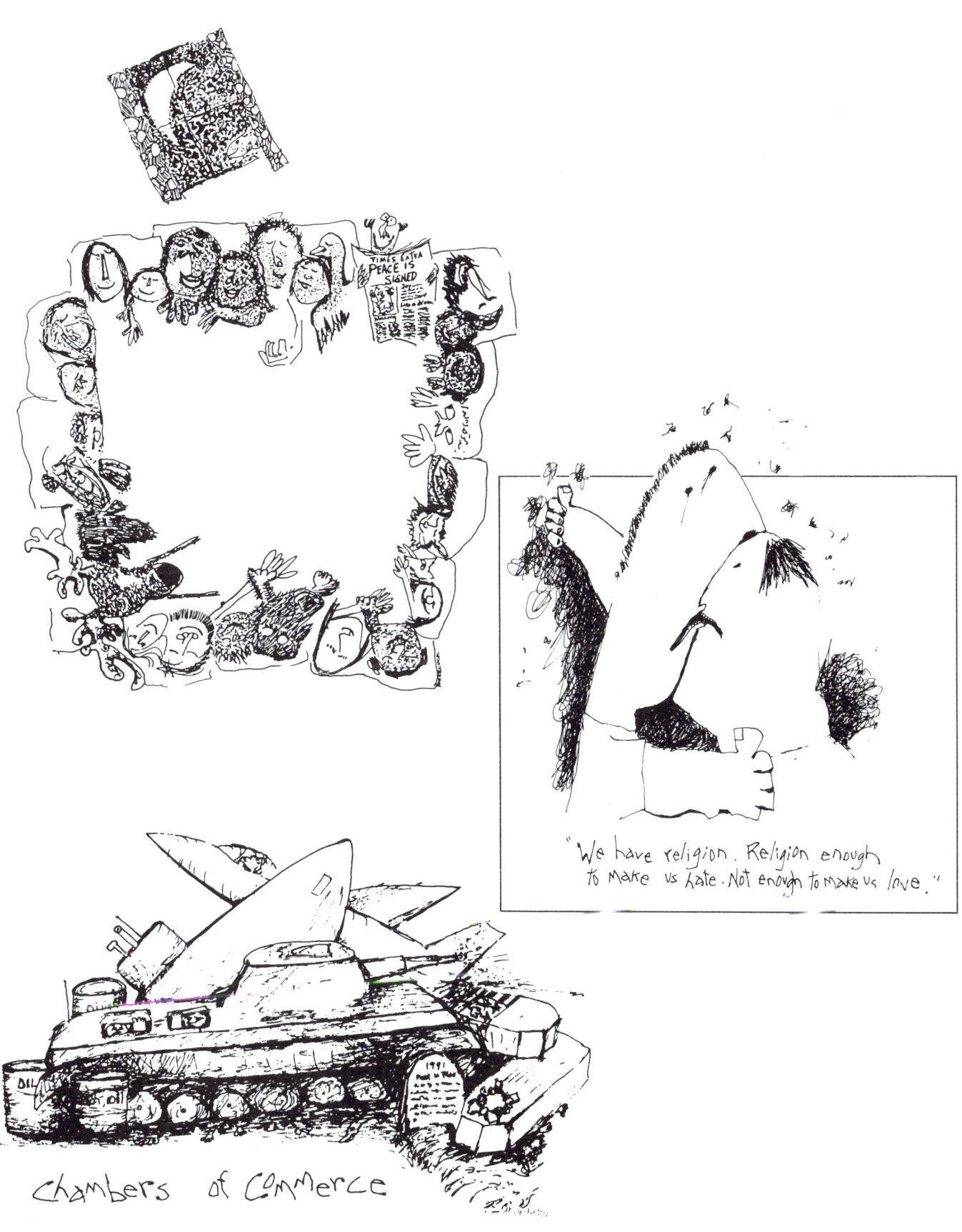

Workshop 1

Justice issues. Protect this. Change this. Stop that. One darn thing after another.

If you can't fix things once and for all — I say why bother?

But do I eat once and for all ... or wash ... or shovel snow once and for all?

Most of life isn't once and for all. Most of it is again and again.

I wish I was a stone. A stone is once and for all.

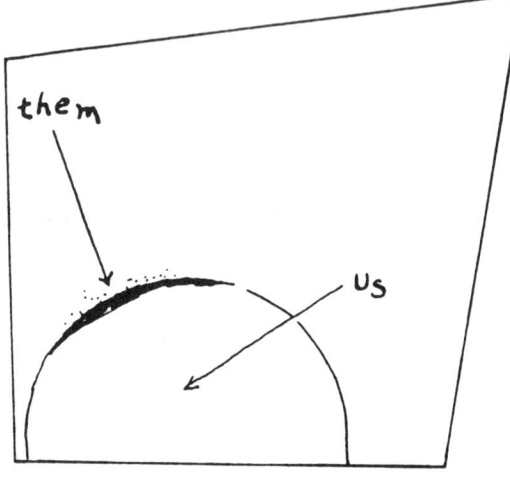
The Russians, being cunning and devious, hide their country behind the curve in the earth so we can't see. We, on the other hand, are right out in the open on the flat part.

Patient suffering from a military-industrial complex

12 Love Your Enemies

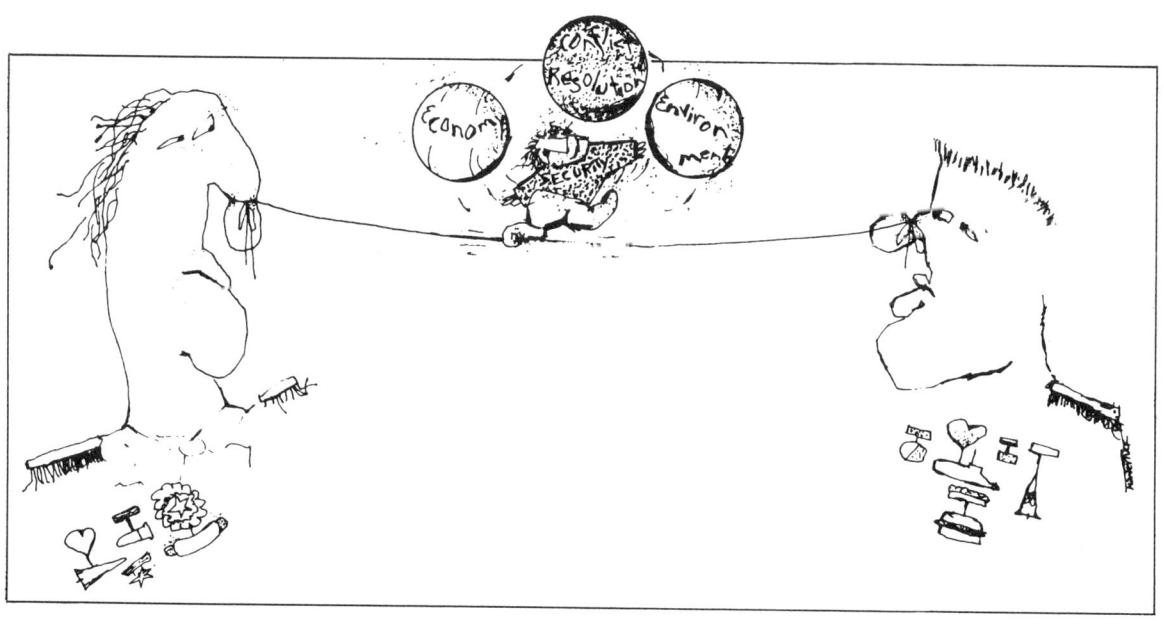

Musings

Teach your children what we have taught our children, that the earth is our mother. Whatever befalls the earth, befalls the children of the earth. If we spit upon the ground, we spit upon ourselves. This we know. The earth does not belong to us; we belong to the earth....

One thing we know, which the white man may one day discover – our God is the same God. You may think that you own Him as you wish to own our land; but you cannot. He is the God of all people, and His compassion is equal for all. This earth is precious to God, and to harm the earth is to heap contempt on its Creator....

So love it as we have loved it. Care for it as we have cared for it. And with all your strength, with all your mind, with all your heart, preserve it for your children, and love ... as God loves us all.
– *Chief Seattle, Squamish Nation, 1854.*

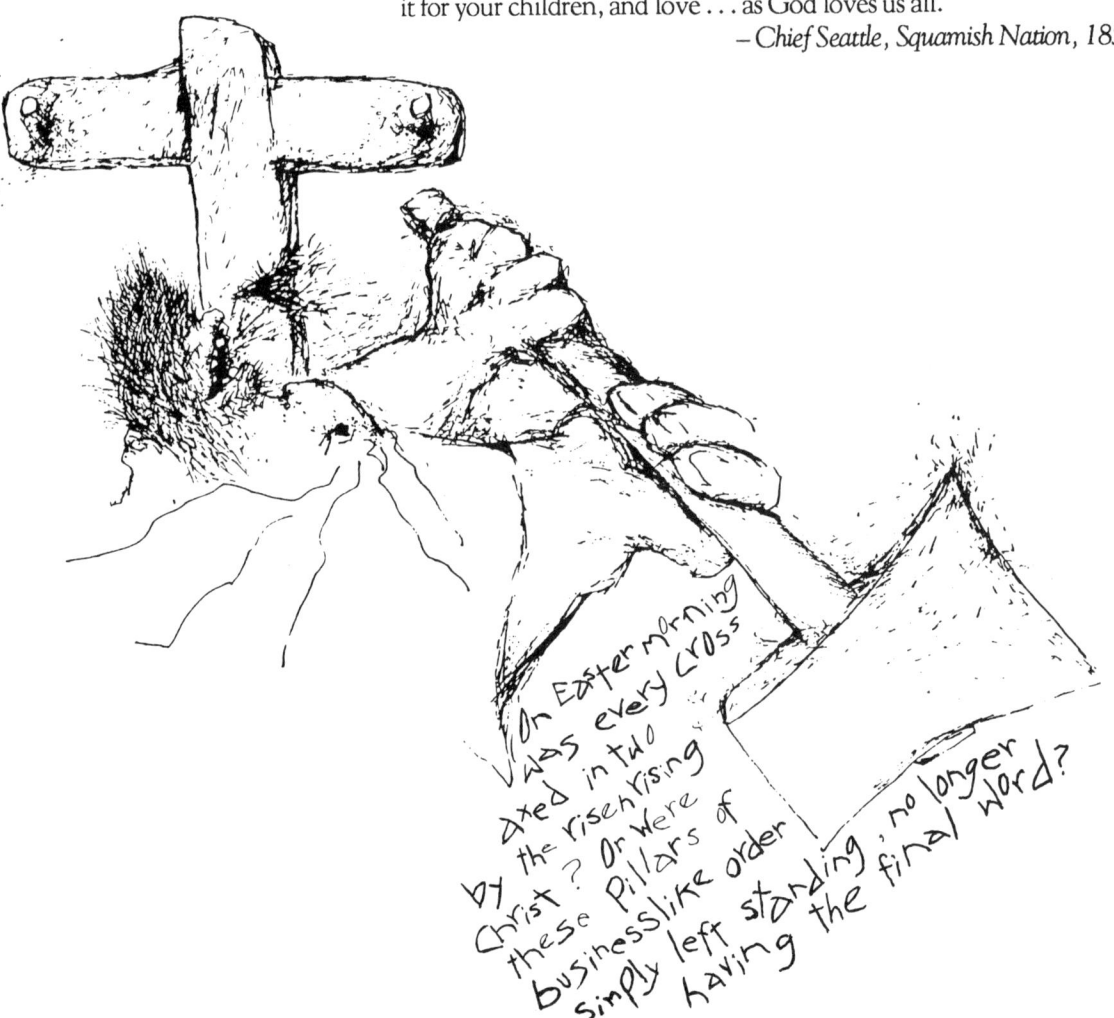

On Easter morning was every cross axed in two by the risen Christ? Or were these pillars of businesslike order simply left standing, no longer having the final word?

Love Your Enemies

Anticipating or Prefiguring What Might Be

... A prefigurative vision adequate to the faith of a nuclear age must penetrate to the chamber of nuclear horror. It cannot merely be a positive image of a transformed society, floating before us like a big security blanket in the sky, or pacifying the video games. No, it needs to grasp the imminence of annihilation to plunge into the abyss before it rises. Unless vision holds on to the actual prospect of doom embodied in the Trident, it cannot transcend that doom, but will slide off into banality and become inadequate to hope. Technocracy will prevail once again.

Because they can envisage nothingness and the Apocalypse, religions have come to play a special role in the antinuclear struggle.... Without faith we sink into the tepid realism that goes along with being reasonable.... In fact, one often feels crazy and possessed to hold on to a vision beyond nuclear weapons, in the face of the prodigious efforts made by technocratic society to present itself as sane. The normalization of nuclear terror is a very powerful mechanism and it is never turned off. To keep the faith against it can bear an alarming resemblance to paranoid experience.

... Here is the authentic challenge of faith; both to go down into the abyss and to come up again rejoined with the human universe and the universe as a whole. We may call it the work of Eros, the great force of unification which animates the universe and which is here experienced as hope. The faith of antinuclear politics is a faith that draws Eros to itself out the abyss of annihilation. Then Otherness no longer remains locked away in paranoid projections: it, too rejoins and empowers the self even as the self joins others.

... It would be a mistake ... to expect struggles within the self to recede during the course of the struggle against the state. Instead, the struggle grows, becoming marked with affirmation and the ascension of Eros. Because the struggle is perpetual, however, anti-nuclear politics is one of drama and ritualization, even, at times, ecstasy. And its triumph will be known by a new aesthetic as well as by the material reorganization of society.

— *Joel Kovel*

I told him, "We're angels."
He said, "Where are the feathers?"
I said, "We got no bloody feathers — only some message about mercy!"
He said, "I need feathers."
I said, "Will you settle for someone with black hair and a guy four feet tall?"
"Okay," he said.
And I gave him the message.

WORKSHOP 2

Crying over spilled milk: rising up against injustice, war, and the disintegration of creation.

Our first workshop focussed on envisioning a state of well-being for all creation. We begin with such visions, not assuming that we do live in such a state, but assuming that we do not. Dismantled optimism is the ground wherein visions of "hope" may grow.

This workshop sets out to uncover our sense of failed hope and optimism. In time, we will examine in detail key problem areas for peaceworkers such as the dogma of the "big stick," militarism, and economic interests. However, we begin by giving voice to a whole range of dangers and wrongs that need to be verbalized. We do this recognizing that the greater our hope, the greater our courage to look, speak and feel.

It is important to articulate, to give form to the feelings that arise when we look at injustice and suffering. Scripture, in its wisdom, would have us understand "seeing" as a matter of the heart, no less than of the eye or the intellect. This realization is crucial for peacemakers and it needs to become a routine response. For this reason, we shall spend time learning to see and speak with our heads *and* our hearts.

Objectives:
- To re-establish everyone's sense of welcome and to continue the building of trust.
- To playfully make our way into some difficult subject matter.
- To encourage an exchange of thoughts and feelings about the most pressing examples of injustice and violence.
- To experience ritual as a deep expression of our faith.
- To consider the wisdom of giving voice to sorrow.

PART A

(10 min.)

Activity 1
The following is a meditative exercise. When leading this, you should speak softly and clearly. Give time between each step for people to do what you are suggesting.

We are going to begin this session with a period of meditation. Would everyone find a comfortable sitting position? You might try sitting in your chair with your back straight, feet on the floor, and hands resting on your thighs. You may choose to sit on the floor. I am going to suggest a means of relaxing. Follow me if you find it helpful.

Close your eyes. Become aware of your breathing. Slowly draw in a deep breath and hold it. Now let it out slowly. Breathe in slowly, deeply, hold it. Now, let it out slowly. As you exhale, squeeze out every last breath from down deep. Continue your slow, deep breathing for a while. Focus on the sound of your own breathing.

(After two minutes . . .) Bring into your mind's eye one of the images of peaceableness that engaged you in our last session, or in your meditation work since we last met. Hold on to that image. Imagine the sounds that might come from it. Imagine the smells. Imagine the feel/touch of each figure. Are there tastes to savour? If you are not already part of the scene, imagine yourself walking into it, being welcomed, and finding a place. Spend a while enjoying your place there. (After four or five minutes . . .) Now imagine telling the people there that you must leave, but that you will return. Imagine walking away, stopping to turn and waving goodbye. Return now to your breathing. When you're ready, open your eyes.

Would some of you like to share briefly how your meditation went?

(35 min.)

Activity 2
Have individuals look through the cartoons on the themes of "injustice, violence, and destruction in creation" at the end of the workshop. Ask them to perform the following task and then to answer the questions, which will help unfold the meaning of the cartoons.

First, try to make a sound or sounds that express what you feel as you look at each cartoon. Second, try to name the feeling or feelings each cartoon stirs in you. Write the feelings down before moving on to the next step. Third, what feelings do the cartoons arouse when considered all together? Perhaps it is numbness. Write it down. Finally, what place do anger and sorrow have in the feelings sparked by the cartoons?

After everyone has had enough time alone, invite them to form groups of three or four and to discuss what is uppermost in their minds.

PART B

(10 min.)

Activity 1

In order to prepare for the following exercise, introduce the themes to be explored. The introduction might go along these lines. (Incidentally, my retelling of the Balaam story is an attempt to simplify scriptural texts combining several versions of the story, which are at points contradictory. This retelling builds on God's anger with Balaam, and it goes against the interpretation that Balaam is being wholly faithful to God in giving in to King Balaak's request.)

A lovely piece of comedy in the Old Testament is the story of the prophet Balaam and his talking donkey (Num. 22ff). The time is about 1200 B.C., shortly after six o'clock. Balaam is a prophet of renown. It is believed that he gives powerful blessings and curses and that he sees visions.

Balaam is for hire, and hired he is by the king of one of the fortress cities that block the Hebrews' entrance into Canaan. God is not happy with Balaam. God sends an angel to block Balaam's way through the mountain. This prophet, or seer, does not see the angel but his donkey does. Balaam sees better with his donkey's head than with his own – even if he doesn't look any better. This is how the comedy begins.

In the easily-misused Psalm 8, humankind is spoken of as superior to every creature and only "a little lower than the angels." Balaam's donkey is just one of many reminders that the earth's creatures, for all their apparent lowliness, and also the earth itself, see God's angels and give voice to God's ways when proud, heaven-gaping humans do not. God's nerve ends, as it were, extend throughout creation, and creation includes all forms of life. So when humans, especially the powerful, are not just and merciful, all of creation suffers and dies. Isaiah speaks of a nation where justice and mercy are of no real concern: "The earth is mourning, pining away . . . the earth is defiled" (Is. 24:4ff).

Jeremiah, too, is poetic (or is it realistic?) when speaking of the wicked idolatry of national security: "How long will the land be in mourning, and the grass wither all over the countryside? The animals and birds are dying as a result of the wickedness of the inhabitants" (Jer. 12:4).

The earth is sensitive to the cruelty of humans and Nature alike. Job, in defending himself against accusations of injustice, insists that he has never overworked the land, or caused the earth suffering, or made it "run with tears" (Job 31:38). Since the earth and animals are often victimized along with the poor, we need laws to protect them all. The purpose of the "Sabbath," for example, was in part to assure rest for the poor, the land, and the animals. Likewise the seventh year, and the year following seven times seven years, the Jubilee year . . . the time of liberation. Entwined in this key biblical fabric is a theology of ecology, mercy, and justice.

It seems clear that what we call Nature and what scripture calls creation is entwined with and dependent on human action for good or ill. Perhaps the injustice of the powerful toward the powerless ultimately registers in nature. The human domination of the rest of creation reflects a similar order – or rather, disorder.

(70 min.)

Activity 2

We have a list of Old and New Testament passages that focuses on the interplay between injustice, violence and the abuse of creation. The texts to be considered often come from stories that are hundreds of years apart. Nevertheless, certain themes persist.

Our task is to read the passages with the following questions in mind:

- *In each case, what is the cause of suffering?*

- *Who suffers in each instance? Are those who suffer connected to one another?*

- *Are your thoughts and feelings about injustice and violence addressed by any of these readings? If so, how? If not, can you say why not?*

The texts to be considered are: Genesis 4:1-12; Leviticus 26:33-36; Isaiah 14:3-10; Jeremiah 5:23-28; Hosea 4:1-3; Matthew 27:45-51; Romans 8:18-22.

Allow for twenty-five minutes of individual work before having people work for fifteen minutes or so in pairs. Focus particularly on number three of the suggested questions.

Another forty minutes should be allowed for the whole group to explore the same question.

PART C

(35 min.)

Worship

The worship takes place either in a circle on the floor marked with a table cloth or around a table. In front of each person is a small glass of water, a spoon, a small plate, and a chunk of brown bread torn from an uncut loaf.

If you use the form of psalm-reading proposed, there is wisdom in explaining the idea before worship begins. Of course, it should be practised by you and the reader beforehand. The instruction might sound like this:

After the words of gathering for worship, there will be a somewhat unusual psalm reading. We all join in this reading by making the sound of a heartbeat. "Jack" will start us off by tapping his hand above his heart with the rhythm of a heartbeat. We will join in rhythm. "Donna" will then read the Psalm, working within the heartbeat rhythm.

1. Words of Gathering:

Now let us be gathered before the Holy One, who becomes the lowly one in Christ, our brother; and hope becomes a sister to us in the Holy Spirit.

2. After Jack leads the group into the unified heartbeat, Donna reads Psalm 130.

3. A Ritual of Sorrow:

In front of us is a glass of blessing, a glass of water. The water may remind us of the refreshing waters bursting from the rock in the desert where Moses and the people walked for so long. It may remind us of the gospel image of Christ. He is seen as "the living water" who will make all things new, even the hard and stony world and the all-too-silent heavens. The water may also remind us of Christ's tears or God's tears, of which Jeremiah spoke:

> For the wound of the daughter of my people wounds me too,
> all looks dark to me, terror grips me.
> Is there no balm in Gilead any more? Is there no doctor there?
> Then why does it make no progress,
> this cure of the daughter of my people?
> Who will turn my head into a fountain,
> and my eyes into a spring for tears,
> so that I may weep all day, all night,
> for all the dead out of the daughter of my people?
>
> (Jer. 8:21-23)

With these reminders of God's grace come hearts better able to feel, eyes better able to see and to cry tears for the sorrows. Let us now take the time in God's presence to name some of the sources of sorrow around us and in us. As each sorrow is named, dip your spoon into your glass of sweet water and empty it onto your plate. As the sources of sadness are spoken, our cup is made less . . .

4. When the glasses are emptied or when everyone is finished speaking, and after a reasonable period of silence, the following meditation may be used.

A short meditation on the wisdom of weeping:

Early on in Shakespeare's King Lear, *Lear finds himself increasingly hurt and bewildered by the growing coldness and cruelty of his powerful children. He is close to a breakdown. He confides in his companion, a loyal clown:*

> ... You think I'll weep; no, I'll not weep.
> I have full cause of weeping: but this heart
> shall break into a hundred thousand splinters,
> or ere I'll weep. O fool, I shall go mad.

Lear refuses tears, which he calls "women's weapons." He doesn't weep; he goes mad. Madness is but one possible cost of not speaking about deep sorrow.

It is natural to feel sadness in response to being hurt or to seeing the hurt and pain of others. Lear allows part of his sadness to fuel his anger, and he buries the rest. Feeling only anger in place of sadness is a common reaction; more so among males, it seems. It is also common to turn or deflect our attention from these things, and to busy ourselves with work, family, home or entertainment. This way there is no time to see or feel what God turns us toward. Especially effective is the way we busy ourselves with things that have some virtue attached: "It's because I'm busy taking care of my family that I have no time whatsoever."

Over time, we become like burn victims. We dread being touched or touching lest it cause more dreaded pain. We clothe ourselves in an armour of indifference and dullness. The less we feel, the less we'll feel pain. We commonly hide our pain, which prevents healing, and makes us incapable of feeling joy. Unfortunately, this behaviour is all too common.

The biblical stories and songs would send us in a different direction. Crying before God and to God is what crisis and confusion call forth. Whether it's Hagar with her dying child, Israel under Pharaoh's mega-projects, the psalm-singing David, the prophet Jeremiah, or Jesus himself – the tears roll down like a mighty river.

Failing to distinguish between whining and crying, our society retorts: "If you can't change it – right away – shut up about it," or, "Don't just cry. Do something!" or "Nothing can be done about it, so why cry about it?"

Again and again, scripture says, "When it seems that nothing can be done about the anguish, cry. Cry to God and only in the crying will you know whether, in fact, anything can be done." By crying before God, we come to see more clearly, through tear-washed eyes, what the situation is, and what, through God's grace, it may come to be. Eyes that have not cried are less able to see what may be done, or even to clearly see what the situation is. It is false to think of crying as inactivity. Grieving tears are part of the rhythm of listening and speaking and listening to God and to one another. They are an inevitable part of seeking God's peace and justice.

Recall, in the Gospel of Luke, how Jesus walked up to the walls of the Holy City. There he stopped and began to weep at its refusal of grace, at its religiosity hiding injustice, at its order without mercy, at its pretended peace rooted in violence and death. Jesus cried out in pain. And then he went into the heart of the city and cried out against the causes of the pain, overturning the money-changers' tables. In scripture, crying before God often precedes spirited action by the weepers and the World-Mender. Weeping is part of the rhythm of prayer and graceful action.

Finally, a word about hearts that feel the suffering of the world and of creation. Hearts that hurt already contain a grain of hope. If our hearts were hopeless, if there were no possibility of improvement, there would be nothing troubling about the pervasiveness of injustice, cruelty, and pain. The crisis would be as natural and as ordinary as gravity. But, to feel the sin and stupidity of our plight is to sense already God's grace and God's "yes" to a world of mercy, which, so far, we refuse.

We may only "see" this graceful love in fleeting glimpses. Yet as Leonard Cohen sings, it is "a love so vast and shattered, it will reach you everywhere." We know God's grace in bits and pieces: a glass of water, a plate of tears, a piece of bread, broken for us.

Take a moment now in your own hearts to name and to give thanks to God for the bits and pieces of grace that you do see in your lives.

Now, in thanksgiving, for the gift of community where we may share joy and sorrow alike, let us dip our piece of bread in our neighbours' dish of tears; neighbours to one side and to the other. Let us eat our little piece of bread and drink our little glass of water. To the well-fed and the well-to-do, these are as nothing. To those hungry for justice and mercy, they are a feast!

5. Song: "When I Survey the Wondrous Cross."

6. Benediction:

Go now in the company of God
who is beside us
in our sadness,
as well as in our joy and strength.
Go with a blessed unrest. Amen.

When I Survey The Wondrous Cross

Isaac Watts 1674-1748
based on Galatians 6:14

ROCKINGHAM 8 8 8 8
adapted by Edward Miller 1731-1807

1. When I survey the wondrous cross
on which the Prince of glory died,
my richest gain I count but loss,
and pour contempt on all my pride.

2. Forbid it, Lord, that I should boast
Save in the death of Christ, my God:
All the vain things that charm me most
I sacrifice them to his blood.

3. See from his head, his hands, his feet,
Sorrow and love mingled down!
Did e'er such love and sorrow meet,
Or thorns compose so rich a crown?

4. Were the whole realm of nature mine,
That were a present far too small:
Love so amazing, so divine,
Demands my soul, my life, my all.

Workshop 2

the Press conference

we-attack civilians??? | **I'm ashamed of you.** | **you disgust me!**

Look dupe, we destroy military targets, and only military targets!!

military targets

Love Your Enemies

Workshop 2

Musings

Sam and Me: Life with an Abusive Superpower

You can feel it building again. The violence is coming... it's only a matter of time. Watch him carefully, watch his moods, his gestures, anticipate what he wants, agree with whatever he says, walk on eggs, try to stay out of his way... The knot of nerves that is your body is getting tighter.

You've seen it all before. The build-up. The blowup. The violence, directed at whatever is the handiest target: kids, dogs, you – smashing things, smashing people. And even when it's not directed at you, you will always get some of the fall-out. The stakes are getting higher. The violence is getting worse. The place you live in is beginning to feel like a war zone.

What will the pretext be this time? It hardly matters. Try to avert it. Try not to think about it. But you are thinking about it, every minute of every day. Please, let it happen. Let it be over with. Let me be able to sleep, to forget, to hope there's a lull before the next time...

God, it was awful. You hurt all over, and yet you are enveloped in numbness. In the pit of your stomach, you feel a sick disgust. With him. With yourself for letting it happen. For staying with him. He is all sweetness again, placating you. Telling you how much he cares. Telling you to come to bed. You want to crawl into a different bed tonight. But you can't. Don't dare. So you go to him...

Reflection

The pervasive feelings of early and mid-January of 1991 began to seem awfully familiar to me: the unbearable tension, growing fear, the feeling of helplessness which alternated with a sense of anger at being put in this position. Where had I seen this or felt this before? Then, it came to me: all the women, abused, living with violent, tyrannical partners, who had told me their stories.

Even though such abuse is not part of my personal history, I began to see their stories as my story – our story, living with Uncle Sam. The events of the pre-Gulf War period have confirmed for me Canada's position in the configuration of world powers. We have chosen and are choosing, through the decisions of our own conservative government, to stay with our friends/neighbours/partners south of the border, even as we become increasingly fearful and appalled at the violence (incipient and blatant) ingrained in that partner. Surely part of the reason we hang on to this relationship is the same dynamic that motivates many women in abusive relationships; the need for economic security and the unwillingness or inability to contemplate a radically different standard and way of living.

For me, the erosion of our self-esteem and a pervasive sense of shame at our complicity embody a further parallel. Will we, as many courageous women are now doing, find the strength to name the dynamics of this relationship, name the violence, talk with others who feel the same way, and start to work towards a very different future for ourselves and our children?

– *Gerry Haverluck, 1991*

The Mighty lion of Judah, Jesus
he cries
he cries
he cries over the unholy city
that cries not for peace
nor for justice.

Love Your Enemies

Not able to speak
the confusion and sorrow,
the exile sits at home among stones.

On Anothers Sorrow
... He doth give his joy to all.
He becomes an infant small.
He becomes a man of woe
He doth feel the sorrow too.

Think not, thou canst sigh a sigh,
And thy maker is not by.
Think not, thou canst weep a tear,
And thy maker is not near.

O! He gives to us his joy,
That our grief he may destroy
Till our grief is fled and gone
He doth sit by us and moan.
— *William Blake*

The exile waits among stones
with a waiting that is weeping
waits among stones
until the stones smell of bread.

WORKSHOP 3

"Oh ya, but what about the Sama~~ri~~tans? Rus~~si~~ans? Iraqis?": mixed messages in the biblical stories about war and peace.

The Bible does not speak with a single voice about dealing with enemies. And there seems little point in pretending that it does. Inevitably, certain voices are thoughtfully or thoughtlessly given priority and are seen as pivotal; certain texts as weightier than others.

Consider the Elisha stories. When Elisha, God's mouthpiece, is teased by a group of children, he calls forth two bears to seriously chew on them. Yet when a war party of enemy soldiers is captured by Elisha and Israel's soldiers, Elisha counsels mercy. He proposes a feast, and freedom for the prisoners.

The Bible as a whole offers an even more extreme spectrum. It ranges from God calling forth the slaughter of every enemy child, woman, old man, and animal, to God coming to earth as a sacrifice to redeem the murderers and all the people they represent. Christ is sacrificed so that God and humankind might be at peace.

In biblical texts, both sacrificial love and unrestrained brutality can be interpreted as God's will. Which one is at the heart of scripture, and at the heart of God?

This workshop helps us to consider scripture's conflicting interpretations of God's ways. We will spend time exploring the confrontation between Christ, Christ's disciples, and an antagonistic Samaritan village. From this incident we move to a consideration of the crucial implications of biblical interpretation for peacemakers.

Objectives:

- To introduce a more critical use of scripture.
- To address troubling personal thoughts, and feelings of resentment or revenge, in the context of worship.

PART A

(15 min.)

Activity 1

This exercise uses music to help the group rejoin and to warm up for the workshop's main tasks. The music should be quiet and gentle. Instrumental music using a solo guitar or harp, for example, would be suitable. The music should be playing when people arrive.

When ready to begin, ask everyone to find a space that gives them enough room to swing their arms. Since some may feel a little shy about what follows, ask everyone to face away from the group. Have each person turn to the drawing of the dove, propped up on a chair in front of them. Remind the group that, in biblical stories, the dove bearing an olive branch first appears after the terror of the flood. The dove comes to signal the peaceful beginning and the promise of well-being that God gives to all the creatures of the earth. Recall God's bow of water droplets and colour-filled light, a bow without an arrow. A bow bent away from the earth, pointing at the heavens; at God, as it were. Remember the dove, fluttering God's delight at the baptism of Christ, at the baptism of the Prince of Peace.

The task is for everyone to stand comfortably awhile, in the midst of the music. When ready, carefully trace the line of the dove picture in the air with a finger. Then re-draw that line, only on a much larger scale, using your whole arm. Next, use both arms and your swaying body to playfully depict this, or your own, dove image. As people repeat this exercise, ask them to recall some of the past weeks' images of hurt or harm, and of well-being. Invite them to let their bodily gesture of the dove over-reach and encompass those recollected images. End this exercise by asking everyone to let their arms simply rest at their sides and to stand in the music for a few moments longer.

PART B

Study of Luke 9:51-55

We are going to do a tag-team role-play. One team represents the viewpoint that God's enemies – that is, our enemies – should be "slaughtered." This group's representative is "John." The team will be given scriptural passages to support their position. The other team represents the viewpoint that we must seek to turn enemies into friends. They are given readings that ground their position. This group's representative is "Mary."

(15 min.)

Activity 1

After the groups have formed into small circles, read Luke 9:51-55 aloud, twice, and give the background to it.

Workshop 3

Peace

Jesus' home province was Galilee, "Galiha ha Goyim," the district of the pagans. Between Galilee and Jerusalem was the province of Samaria which, like Galilee, was part of the earlier northern kingdom of Solomon's Israel. At the death of Solomon, the tensions between north and south were already great. The south, which included the Holy City of Jerusalem, increasingly saw itself as the true Israel. When the northern kingdom was conquered by Assyria in the eighth century B.C., many of the political, economic, and religious leaders were deported to the ends of the Assyrian empire.

Into the north came leaders from other corners of the empire. The intermixing that occurred, especially in Samaria, only cemented the religious pretensions of the south. When the south was conquered in the sixth century B.C., its leaders were also deported. When King Cyrus let them return in order to rebuild the destroyed Jerusalem, the Samaritans actively opposed his plan. To the Samaritans, Jerusalem and the temple symbolized the error of their southern cousins.

The south destroyed the temple at Mount Gerizim, the Samaritans' holy place, in 128 B.C. By the time of Jesus, the bitterness between Jews and Samaritans was well-established. Although Jesus had previously experienced friendship with the Samaritans, the incident in Luke is aggravated by his journey to the holy centre of the Samaritans' established enemies.

(20 min.)

Activity 2
Each group is given a written copy of their background readings.

John's team: *As background, read a few short passages that may have been familiar to the disciples and to Jesus.*

- *A reading from Moses' guidebook regarding the laws for the people of Israel as they prepare to move into their new homeland after forty years in the desert (Deut. 20:10-18).*

- *A reading from a series of stories about the prophet Elijah. Elijah sees himself confronting a king and the king's men who have betrayed God. The king sends his soldiers to order Elijah to come and speak with him (2 Kings 1:9-16).*

- *A third reading, (1 Samuel 15:1-11), centres on a conflict between Saul and God, arising when King Saul refuses to totally annihilate the enemy.*

Mary's team: *Your readings are from the teachings of Christ (Luke 6:27-38). This is part of the "Sermon on the Plain," which is similar to the "Sermon on the Mountain" (Matt. 5). Note the specific advice Jesus gives regarding the response to inhospitable villagers. Have the group recall the Lord's Prayer and the condition we attach to our request for forgiveness.*

(2 min.)

Activity 3
As teams are preparing, set up a small table in the centre of the room. Place three chairs around it. Once the teams are ready, introduce them to the mechanics of the tag-team role-play.

In tag-team role-play, one member is asked to represent the whole team. As the play proceeds, any team member can replace the current representative by tapping her on the shoulder and then taking her place. As the role-play continues, everyone can have a turn.

(15 min.)

Activity 4
Once everyone understands the mechanics of role-playing, the scene can be set and role-play can begin.

The setting is an inn outside the Samaritan village. Mary has left Jesus to see what has been taking James and John so long. James has gone for a walk. John, who is visibly worried, is having a cold drink at a table. Mary joins him.

(15 min.)

Activity 5
After the role-play has had a chance to develop, have another follower of Jesus enter. She has been sent to see what the hold-up is. However, she ends up asking a new question, if it has not already been asked: "What are we to do when Christ's life and teaching of forgiveness and reconciliation appear to contradict some of scripture?"

(10 min.)

Activity 6
Signal the role-play's end with a call for applause. (The noise may signify praise, and/or a wish to "distance" the drama.) Allow enough time for people to leave behind their assumed roles. Invite actors to describe how their role "felt," and what they learned from the experience.

(25 min.)

Activity 7
After a break, ask people to gather in groups of three or four to discuss two questions. Then have sub-groups share key thoughts with the whole group. The questions are:

- *How do we respond to arguments that use scripture to justify war?*

- *When Jesus rebukes his disciples, does he rebuke our nations for resorting to war (cold or hot) with other nations over interpretations of truth, economic interest, security, and so on?*

PART C

(40 min.)

Worship

The worship should take place in a circle. This worship requires a bowl of vinegar and a bowl of honey, as well as a cross, a candle, or a Bible at the centre.

1. Let us be gathered in prayer:

O Holy Maker and Mender of the Earth and all its peoples,
O Holy Giver of breath and life awhile,
you are Mystery and Mercy both.
Spirit our praise, we pray. Amen.

2. *Listen to some basic truths from St. Paul's letter to a group of Christians in the commercial centre of Colossae. They were a church resigned to the present order of the world: who was in, who was out, what could not be changed, what was already decided – or so it appeared. The world's authorities seemed to have fixed everything in old directions (Col. 1:15-20 and 3:10-15).*

3. Song: "Let There Be Light," verses 1-3.

4. Symbolic action using vinegar and honey, with the following introduction:

In front of us is a dish with honey and a dish with vinegar. In a few moments we will taste each of them. But first, recall that this evening we have explored conflicting understandings of God's will toward Israel's enemies. And this is a conflict, not only between the Old Testament and the New, but a conflict found within both of the Testaments.

For example, in the Book of Kings, Elijah uses fire to burn up his enemy countrymen, whereas Elisha, his successor, counsels against such violence toward enemies. So, when an invading Aramean war party is itself captured while trying to capture Elisha, Elisha responds with: "Do not kill them . . . offer them food and water, so that they can eat and drink, and then let them go back to their master" (2 Kings 6:22f). The king provided a great feast for them; and when they had eaten and drunk, he sent them off and they went back to their master. Aramean raiding parties never invaded the territory of Israel again.

Similarly, in the New Testament there is a conflicting tone and emphasis between the Christ of the pastoral Epistles and the Christ of the Gospels. The pastoral Epistles repeatedly collapse into hard-heartedness toward outsiders, which reveals the church's need to rest more fully in Christ's spirit. Also, the conflict between Peter and James and his Jerusalem church, and that between Paul and Peter over table fellowship with gentiles, shows that Christians, inside and outside of scripture, should not confuse their own

Workshop 3

small notion of mercy with Christ's great mercy. This means – for us, as for Paul – that at times we need to consciously emphasize certain scriptural positions against others.

Such decisions surrounding interpretation cannot be avoided. Regarding treatment of the enemy, for example, God can be claimed to support contradictory positions. Nevertheless, if Christ's love for a humanity at enmity with God is pivotal to our redemption, and to our life-direction as Christians, it is also pivotal to our interpretation of scripture. Christ calls us to resist the tendency to shut the door to his love once we think we are safely inside: "Now I am safe; let revenge and punishment and slaughter begin."

The illusion that our enemies (and not we) are God's enemies is a recurring temptation. The temptation to think that only we, and not others, enjoy God's grace recurs in us as it did in the early church of scripture. If we think that the time has come to stop praying for and loving our enemies, we are the cuckoo in time's clock.

Hard-heartedness toward others, and thereby toward Christ, is a part of us and a temptation from the earliest days of scripture. It is like the vinegar that the soldiers mockingly offer the Christ (Luke). Let us dip our fingers in the bowl of vinegar and touch it to our mouths and, as we taste it, recall our own attraction to getting even or to "teaching them a lesson." Let us recall our own resistance to the wideness of Christ's mercy. (Time for meditation.)

This second bowl is filled with honey. It is a symbol of the blessings of God. Was it not honey along with milk that symbolized God's gift of a dwelling place to the raggedy band who muttered and murmured at Moses for forty years? Was it not honey that helped sustain John the Baptist as he lived on society's edge, telling of the coming Christ? As we dip our fingers into the honey bowl, and swallow some of the honey, let us recall the sweetness of God's mercy in becoming Christ, our brother and our hope. (Time for meditation.)

5. Prayer (to be read slowly):

O Holy Mystery and Mercy,
You are a darkness to our little lights,
and Light to great dark.
To our vinegar hearts, sour with sinning,
your mercy is as honey.
Sweet, yes, but wild as bees.
Yes, and a danger to all plans secured by
violence and terror.
Wild, dangerous, merciful Thou -
may thy Christly commonwealth come. Amen.

6. Song: "Let There Be Light," verses 3-6.

7. Benediction:

*Go now in the good company of God the
Father who mothers us,
Christ our brother
and our sister the Holy Spirit. Amen.*

LET THERE BE LIGHT

CONCORD 4 7 7 6
Robert J.B. Fleming 1921-

1. Let there be light, let there be understanding,
let all the nations gather, let them be face to face;

2. Open our lips
   Open our minds to ponder,
   Open the door of concord
   Opening into grace;

3. Perish the sword,
   Perish the angry judgement,
   Perish bombs and hunger,
   Perish the fight for gain;

4. Hallow our love,
   Hallow the deaths of martyrs,
   Hallow their holy freedom,
   Hallowed be thy name;

5. Thy kingdom come,
   Thy spirit turn to language,
   Thy people speak together,
   Thy spirit never fade;

6. Let there be light,
   Open our hearts to wonder,
   Perish the way of terror,
   Hallow the world God made.

Francis Wheeler Davis 1936-

Love Your Enemies

Musings

Revolutionary Love of our Enemies
... The Sermon on the Mount was authenticated through its preacher. So it is not merely a lofty ideal. It is authenticated in us when we discover that he lived for us, suffered for us and died for us, while we were still enemies and godless (cf.Rom. 5:6,10), and when we live and love from this faith. Nor does God come to us by way of anything less than love for our enemy. God does not ask about good and evil, because even my good is not good before him. God's love seeks the enemy and is perfected in the enemy. If it were not for this, none of us could talk about God's love at all. Apart from this, none of us becomes the child of this God. This is the way Jesus, in his life and death, brought God to us. God's children are enemies who have been overcome. God's children live from a hard and costly love. It cost God the death of the Son. Through him, children of God are liberated from ever narrower spirals of hate in the heart and enmity in the world. They emerge from these prisons and see the sun of a new day, which rises in the morning over the evil and the good, making no distinction between them, but giving life and warmth to everyone. And everyone feels the rain which falls on the just and the unjust, and makes the wilderness of desolation fruitful again – without distinction and beyond good and evil....

... For God's sake, for Christ's sake, let us love our enemies! And that means seeing your enemy as your brother and treating him like your brother. Stop asking what he has done to you or to other people. Ask what he suffers from, and what the sufferings are which are turning him into your enemy. Ask what God wants to do for him – the God who lets his sun rise upon the evil and the good. Ask what Jesus has done for him. Love of the enemy is not a matter for weaklings who are afraid of that enemy. Anyone who is still afraid of his enemy does not know what love is. Love is only something for the person who has been liberated and who no longer lets himself be impressed by his opponent. Love of one's enemy does not want to conquer him, or convert him to one's own views. This kind of love lives together with the enemy, beneath God's sun, beyond good and evil. It carries him into this wider horizon....

... Love of one's enemy can be fatal, as we can see from the fate of Martin Luther King and many other martyrs of our time. It needs endurance and strong nerves to see this way through. It needs continually new liberation from the vicious circles of fear and violence with attract us so strongly. It needs the wide space of God's sun, which warms and sheds its light on the evil and the good. Finally – and this is the price – it requires acceptance of suffering.

– *Jurgen Moltmann*

If you want to see the brave, look at those who can forgive.
If you want to see the heroic, look at those who can love in return for hatred.
– *from the Hindu Scripture, the Bhagavad Gita*

From "A Tale of Two Brothers"

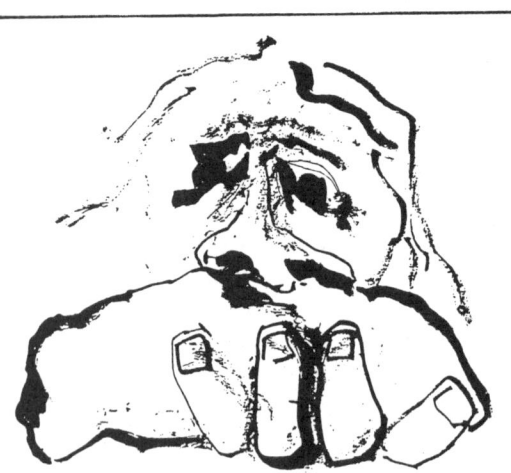

Once upon a time, there was a man named Cain. Cain had an altar of stones, and a brother. And then Cain had no brother, no altar, and one stone. It smelt sweet and was all sticky red.

Is it Abel that Cain wants dead? or God? or himself? or everyone and everything?

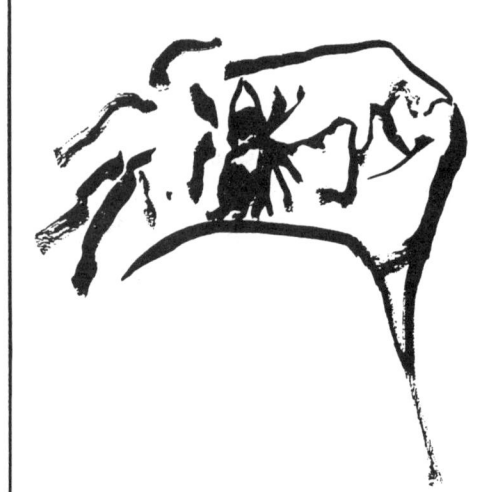

Cain wonders why Abel doesn't get up. Cain is not angry anymore. They could play — if only Abel would get up.

Cain looks God not in the eye and asks, "Am I supposed to be my brother's nursemaid?"

WORKSHOP 4

"Love them? I'd kiss a pig first!": imagining the enemy.

How do we talk about enemies or those whom, in practice, we treat as enemies? How do we imagine them? And those who experience us as enemies. How do they imagine us? What is it that allows some people to see other folks as more than enemies; as precious children of God?

During the time of Jesus, there were religious and political/economic forces that helped shape the way people viewed the world. That world was sharply divided between the so-called righteous and unrighteous, fashioned along lines of the world views presented in such as Leviticus and Ezra. The prevailing frame of reference about the world declared who was "in" and who was "out." Israelite activities were sharply contrasted with non-Israelite activities. The enemy was clothed in the imagery of impurity, uncleanliness, dirt, and so on.

The Christ's acts of healing, his table manners, his choice of table company, as well as his teaching, criticized and undermined the prevailing ethical standards. Love of the enemy was central to Christ's work and to his followers. Imagine love of one's enemies leading folks to live, die, and be resurrected for others!

This workshop encourages us to come to terms with the unsettling enemy that we view as "them," and the enemy that is "us." This will involve facing national enemies, as well as those enemies within our own nation whom we discriminate against because of their race or other distinction.

Objectives:

- To ponder the image of Christ as One who embraces "dirty enemies."
- To identify what makes us enemies to others.
- To address the enmity that exists between the first people of this land and white society.
- To gather in a worship that re-asserts the Christly vision of every race belonging to God's household.

PART A

(10 min.)

Activity 1
This is a centreing exercise using breath control. Have everyone find a comfortable position, sitting with back straight and hands crossed on the lap, or kneeling with back straight and buttocks resting lightly on the heels. Speak in a quiet and clear voice, pausing awhile between each direction.

Be sure your lower back is straight. Let your neck and shoulder muscles relax. Feel your arms relaxing. Let your eyes gradually close. Slowly, blow air out through your mouth. Breathe more air in through your nose and then slowly and steadily blow as much air out as you can from deep inside your lungs. When you think you have exhaled, give a final blow. Now through your nose, draw in fresh air.

Blow out air from deep inside and imagine it making a hole through the walls to the freshness of outside. When you think all the air is blown, give a final puff. Repeat this, slowly and steadily drawing fresh air back in through your nose until it fills your head and your lungs.

When your lungs are filled with new breath, hold that breath a few seconds and let it flow down to your centre just below your navel. Imagine it filling and flowing out through your legs and toes, arms and fingers. Exhale. Repeat this whole process twice.

Now slowly and steadily exhale, blowing your breath through the walls and outdoors. As you draw in fresh air, begin returning to your normal breathing. Slowly open your eyes, registering those around you. When you are ready, stand up slowly.

(5 min.)

Activity 2
The second group rebuilding exercise involves a litany. To break the traditional pattern that suggests that the leader has the answers and the people, the questions, we have given this litany a different arrangement. It should be repeated three times: once, at normal volume; once, loudly; and once, in a whisper.

Leader: Let the people begin.

People: When will we know that night has turned to morning?

Leader: When cranberry bushes are no longer mistaken for spruce trees?

People: Even then, it will not be morning.

Leader: When the sun is warm upon the face?

People: Even then, it will not be morning.

Leader: When, when will night become morning?

People: When in all enemy faces we recognize precious children of God.
       When we recognize sisters and brothers in all faces,

Leader and People: Only then will night have turned to morning.
Amen.

PART B

(30 min.)

Activity 1
This exercise works with the drawing of Christ kissing the pig. Its creator sees the drawing as one interpretation of Christ's love for the enemy. Whether this is a reasonable interpretation will be the task of the group to decide.

People are asked to work in groups of three or four to consider the drawing of Jesus and the pig in light of the following readings: Matthew 5:1-4, 15:21-28, 21:21-35; Luke 5:29-32, 7:36-47; and Romans 5:6-10. After the group has had time to consider the drawing in relation to the texts, ask them to identify the believers, the teachings, and the practices that appear to discourage Jesus from being merciful.

(25 min.)

Activity 2
The next exercise works with the depiction of Christ holding up a pig for a would-be follower to kiss. After everyone has looked at the drawing, ask all of them to "imagine themselves as the pig that Jesus is holding up for one of your enemies to kiss." (This exercise presupposes that we not only have enemies, but that we are enemies to others, for good or bad reasons.)

Participants are next asked to:

- *Think. To whom are you an enemy? Think impersonally, in terms of your inherited role as a citizen of this nation, or as a relatively privileged member of this society.*

- *Are there actions of repentance you could make, thereby making yourself a little more kissable? What might these actions be?*

After individual work is done, ask folks to work in pairs awhile, before a sampling of responses is taken from the whole group.

(50 min.)

Activity 3
This exercise entails working within a fantasy framework. Everyone is asked to imagine that they have been asked, as individuals or in pairs, to prepare a design for a day-long meeting between "our church" and members of an aboriginal/Native church. "We" will be preparing for the day in cooperation with representatives of the Native church. In anticipation of the planning meeting with the aboriginal planners, your task is to do some preparatory thinking. While obviously not wanting to presume to pre-plan everything, a certain amount of prior thought and organization is necessary. To help give some direction to the brooding, a text, Matthew 5:20-26, and a few questions are offered.

Workshop 4

Jesus kisses the unclean.
The protectors of morality
and might are outraged.

Armed with mercy, Christ points a loaded pig at those armed with fear.

The questions are:

- *What might be two or three goals of such a meeting?*
- *What specifically could be done to fulfil these goals in terms of meeting place, atmosphere, activities together, and so on?*
- *What do you not know? What do you need to find out?*
- *What hopes or fears do you bring to such a meeting?*

After twenty-five minutes or so, folks gather again in a circle. All name one response that they had to the first question, the second, and so on. Encourage them to withhold discussion and to only ask questions of clarification of one another until everyone has made a contribution.

PART C

(50 min.)

Worship

Worship will take place around a common meal of representative foods from different nations that we label enemies or friends. For example: wild rice or bannock from the aboriginal community, falafel from Iraq, cabbage rolls from Russia, bean curd from China, apple pie from the United States, and so on. The group can decide which foods to use. Foods should be cut up into small pieces so that when they are served, each person receives just a morsel. This will symbolize the fact that the meal is just an appetizer, a sign of hope, a taste of things to come. Our meal, symbolizing all the nations eating together in peace, is meant to echo the biblical image of peace and of fellowship.

1. Words of Gathering:

Let us be gathered in thanksgiving before the God who lends us breath awhile, turns swords into ploughshares, spears into meat skewers, and our cold, folded arms into loving arms able to embrace all of ragged creation.

2. *Listen to a secret that needs be no secret at all. Listen to God speaking in Paul's letter to an early community of Christians hobbled and tongue-tied by great and tiny fears: Hebrews 2:8-9, 14-18.*

3. *In silence, let us each open the closed window of our heart to God's Spirit in prayer.*

4. Song: "Cana Wine."

5. Reading: Acts 10:1-23.

6. Meditation:

At the centre of our reading is Peter's refusal to eat what God puts before him. God doesn't threaten Peter with no dessert if Peter doesn't eat up. Instead, God addresses Peter's excuse that "I have never yet eaten anything profane or unclean."

Peter, faithful to the religion of his fathers and a legalist in his reading of Leviticus 11, knows that God has holy laws that say if you eat snakes and herons and a hundred other things you become unclean and disgusting. It's in scripture. Peter knows that. Why doesn't God know that?

The teaching of scripture in which God is so central – is wrong, says God. Every kind of animal, reptile, and bird, God has made clean. Being able to recite scripture verses to the contrary is not good enough.

But why were these creatures understood to be unclean in the first place? In part, some were eaten by Israel's enemies or they were associated with religious sacrifice and imagery of Israel's enemies. To eat or to take these creatures into oneself was also to absorb their meanings and associations. Similarly, when we swallow the bread and wine at communion, we swallow the story that this is, in a sense, Christ's body and blood. To eat the esteemed creatures of the enemy was to swallow their stories, which Israel considered religiously unclean and politically dangerous. Eating was and is more than just a matter of nutrition. The outcasts who ate and drank with Jesus knew that food also involved religion and politics.

For us, eating the foods of friends and enemies is also significant. It goes without saying that the significance is not merely a culinary adventure. Rather, it represents a foretaste, and a rehearsal for the time when friendly and enemy nations shall come together in festive meals of celebration. For us it is a sign of the hope expressed in St. John's dream vision:

> Then the angel showed me the river of life, flowing from
> under the throne of God and of the Lamb and flowing
> crystal clear, down the middle of the city street.
> On either bank of the river were the trees of life ... the
> leaves of which are for the healing of the nations.
> (Revelation 22:1-2)

Because we do not know that the healing of the nations will occur, we can only hope that it will happen. Nevertheless, in a world drained by despair, hope is no small thing. As we taste each morsel of food, let us declare in unison after we have savoured each symbol:

> In Christ, we hope for the nations' mending
> not for their slaughter but for their healing.

7. *Let us begin our meal now with a toast to Christ Jesus, our brother and hope:*

A toast to Christ crucified and risen, in whom we are assured that Tyrant death does not have the last word. To Christ!

8. *Following the meal is the litany of blessing first used in a mass in rural Manitoba in the autumn of 1983. Incidentally, some folks miss the fact that the eagle and the bear are not intended to symbolize aboriginal tribes but rather the United States of America and Russia.*

Leader: May terrors shrink to harmless toys
with tyrants fenced like little boys
Pin-striped suits and judges gowns
only worn by circus clowns.

People: May justice and mercy kiss.

Leader: May battles be ball games
And everyone play
And generals kiss
at the end of the day.

People: May justice and mercy kiss.

Leader: May the nations such as
eagle and bear
lose claw and tearing beak
learn meekness and shame
and how to blush again.

People: May justice and mercy kiss.

Leader: May babes, brown and white
milk mouthed be happy
as calves tickled by thistles
licking honey from the sun
licking honey from the sun.

People: May justice and mercy kiss.

Leader: May war be a memory
and prisoners run free
children dancing
old people playing
prophets without call
Everyone singing
the joy of creation
God's love of it all.

Leader and People: Justice and mercy will kiss.

9. Song: "Walk on By."

10. Benediction:

Invite each person to shake the hand of, or to embrace each other person and say, *"May the Peace of Christ be yours now and for evermore."* Amen.

Walk On By
(For those who walk in peace)

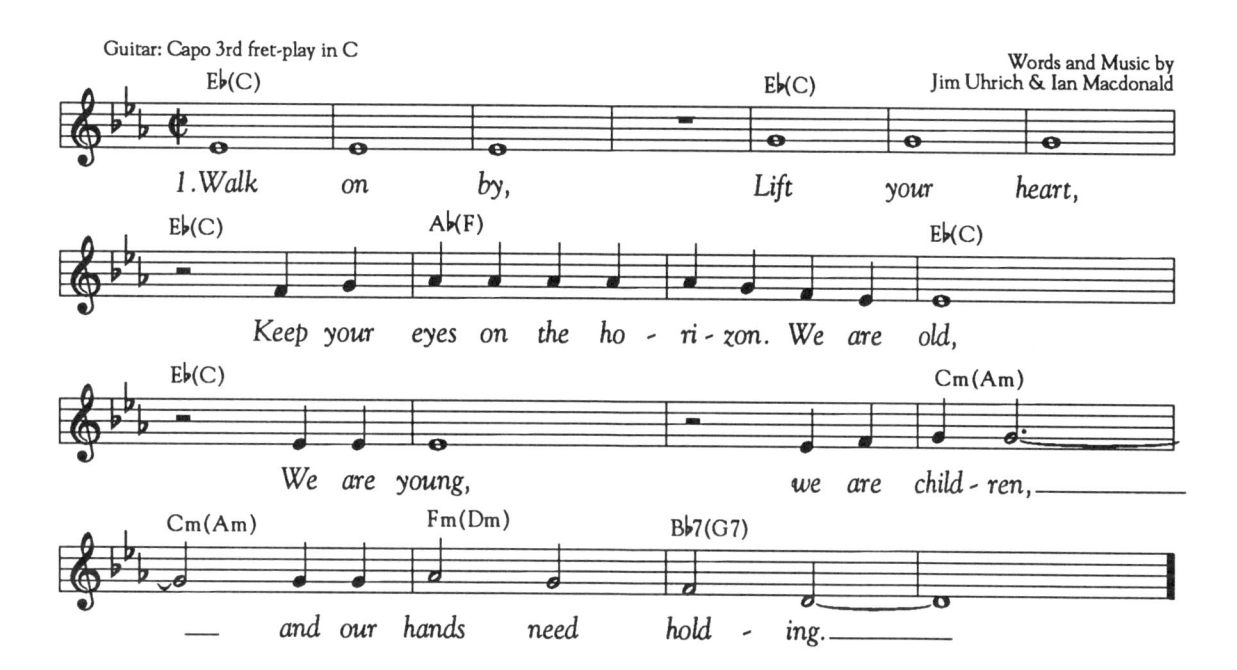

Guitar: Capo 3rd fret-play in C

Words and Music by
Jim Uhrich & Ian Macdonald

1. Walk on by, Lift your heart,
   Keep your eyes on the ho-ri-zon.
   We are old, We are young,
   we are child-ren,
   and our hands need hold-ing.

2. Walk on by, Lift your heart,
   Keep your eyes on one another.
   We are weak, we are strong,
   We are earth's children and the earth's our mother.

3. Walk on by, Lift your heart,
   Keep your eyes on peace and justice.
   We are one, we are many,
   We are children and we love our planet.

4. Walk on by, Lift your heart,
   Keep your eyes on peace and blessing.
   We are old, we are young,
   We are children and our hands are joining.

5. Walk on by, Lift your heart,
   Keep your lives on peaceful pathways.
   We are one, we are many,
   Children walking for a new world rising.

   Repeat first verse

© Common Cup Company, Inc., 271 Queenston Street, Winnipeg, Manitoba R3N 0W9.
Used by permission.

Workshop 4

Musings

At one point in the history of the Lakota-Sioux, the rivalry between the Lakota and the settlers arriving in the country was very intense. The Lakota people were hunted and hanged in large numbers.

At one of these times a group of Lakota men who were in captivity sang in their own language as they walked across the grounds of the fort to the gallows. Most of the people who held them captive and were about to execute them assumed they were singing a pagan song.

The hymn they were singing is now recorded in the *Songs for a Gospel People* (#80). It has a distinct drum beat reflective of the Lakota tradition. It is significant that this misunderstanding of history would be marked in this way by a hymn with these words:

1. Many and great, O God, are your works,
   maker of earth and sky.
   Your hands have set the heavens with stars,
   your fingers spread the mountains and plains.
   Lo, at your word the waters were formed;
   deep seas obey your voice.

2. Grant unto us communion with you,
   O star abiding One.
   Come unto us and dwell with us,
   with you are found the gifts of life.
   Bless us with life that has no end,
   eternal life with you.
   Ka-ti-pe-yi etc.

   – *The Rev. Stan McKay*

Jerusalem, Jerusalem, you that kill the prophets and stone those who are sent to you! How often have I longed to gather your children together, as a hen gathers her brood under her wings, and you refused!... If you...had only recognized on this day the way to peace.

Love Your Enemies

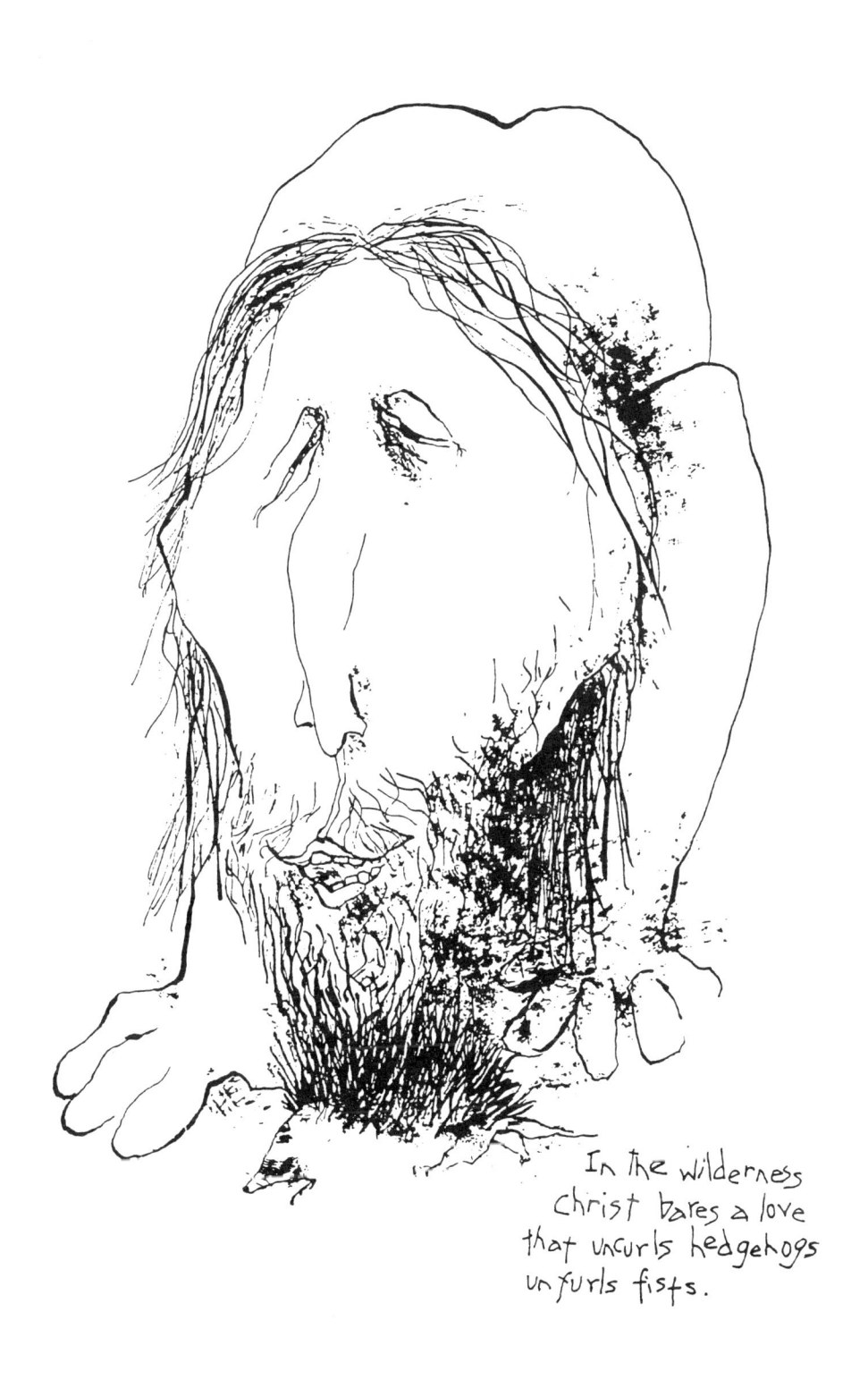

In the wilderness
Christ bares a love
that uncurls hedgehogs
unfurls fists.

Musings

WORKSHOP 5

Turn the cheek; turn the tables; turn direction: loving the powerful by opposition.

"I will love you by opposition," says poet/songwriter Sydney Carter, and, in so saying, he captures one of Christ's many approaches to the love of the enemy. At times, Christ loved by distancing himself from confrontation through gentleness, compassion, or indirect and humorous parables, or sharp pinches of satirical speech; or, at times, by forceful or provocative action.

This workshop introduces the idea of using gesture – such as "turning the other cheek" to a powerful and unjust enemy – as a creative provocation. Christ intended such illustrations to stimulate creative, loving, and nonviolent resistance to wrong, rather than to encourage capitulation or masochism. In the context of the gospel and of this workshop, "love the enemy" means deepening our understanding so that we can more creatively respond to situations of injustice and violence.

Objectives

- To link peace and justice.
- To gain a deeper sense of the forms that love of enemies may take.
- To acknowledge in worship our need of grace for works of love.

PART A

(12 min.)

Activity 1

The following warm-up exercises may be done "straight." My own method is to locate them in a playful fantasy or visualization. I base this exercise on the premise that when you share laughter, you share community. In that regard, it's much like tears. You may wish to invent your own creative visualization for the following.

Before we begin the fantasy, folks should be seated in a circle with their side to the centre of the circle and their front to the next person's back. This will facilitate the massage-like activities that follow.

1. *In a moment, you are going to get a sense of what people who dwell in Saskatchewan's Qu'Appelle Valley experience most summer evenings: fat raindrops on their head and shoulders. Each evening the inhabitants go down to the shores of Echo Lake and sit in a position identical to the position you are in now. When the fat raindrops do not start to gently fall with a tap, tap on head and shoulders and back, they improvise. They slowly raise their hands in front of their faces, spread out their fingers, then bend the fingers slightly downward toward the palm. Next, they begin to imitate the awaited rainfall.*

First the rain comes down slowly, dancing on head and shoulders. Then it comes more quickly, and for just a moment, it pours down onto back, shoulders and head. It then becomes lighter and lighter until it stops. And then everyone turns around to give their chubby raindrop present to the person behind him or her.

2. *Earlier in the day, another ritual is enacted throughout the Qu'Appelle Valley summers. Everyone saunters down and sits in the lake, a few feet from shore. They sit exactly like you're sitting now. There they wait for the golden colour of a school of guppies, the "Toothless Prairie" variety. On the backs, shoulders, and upper arms of the people immersed in the water to their chins, the Toothless Guppies massage their lips and gums. But sometimes the guppies don't arrive and the people must improvise. They raise their hands and bend their fingers to form the outline of the mouth of the Prairie Toothless. They then proceed to massage those in front of them, much as the guppies would, had they appeared. Then the people turn around in order to return the present of the "Guppy Massage."*

3. *The final ritual from the Qu'Appelle Valley is a winter ritual. The people go down to the shore of Echo Lake and sit in a circle with their hands joined. They don't spend a lot of time waiting for the rain, and the guppies have generally swum south for the winter. Conversation is at a low ebb. But everyone simply sits quietly, holds hands, closes their eyes, and listens to the breathing. Each person breathes more deeply and slowly.*

Then someone squeezes the hand of the person beside them, and that hand squeeze is passed around the circle. A second person starts a squeeze and the two are passed on, one after the other. They speed up. And slow down. Stop. Then eyes open and smile. The ritual is ended.

PART B

(25 min.)

Activity 1

In preparation for the groups' work they should be introduced to a reinterpretation of a crucial passage from the Sermon on the Mount, found in Matthew 5:39-40. In order to make this somewhat lengthy presentation more lively and memorable, two playful persons from the group should be drafted to help the narrator. Their responsibility will be to mime the two incidents that the narrator unfurls, using these, or the narrator's own voice. (My reading of the text owes a debt to Walter Wink, *Violence and Nonviolence in South Africa: Jesus' Third Way*, New Society Publishers, Philadelphia, 1987.)

Jesus responds to different people and groups of people in different ways. He speaks no harsh words against the poor, but he does speak out against the religious and politically powerful. Jesus says nothing against atheists and little against Gentiles.

Jesus counsels different actions for people in different positions of power. Jesus counsels the rich young man to become poor and act generously. "Sell" what you have and "give" the money to the poor. Christ also guides the young man (and us) toward what allows him to let go of economic security and social privilege, toward an alternate source of "security" – "come, follow me."

Christ's friendship with Zaccheus also addresses economic power. Zaccheus celebrates Christ's mercy by using his economic power to show mercy toward the poor. But most of Jesus' listeners were the poor in economic, political, social, and religious terms. Without the poor and their suffering in mind, it is easy to misinterpret much of the Sermon on the Mount.

The Sermon's call to love enemies, in terms of "turn the other cheek," for example, has mistakenly been understood as not resisting evil. The King James translators mistranslated a crucial portion to read, "Resist not evil." The Good News Bible is more accurate in its "Do not take revenge on someone who wrongs you." This is to say, "Do not return evil for evil, tit for tat. Do not take revenge or become filled with vengeance. Act out of your freedom as a Child of God." This is not a call for inaction. It is advice on the spirit and direction of action in the face of violence, exploitation, and so on. It is not a command to do nothing. It is counsel on how to do what must be done, resisting evil and working toward a peaceable community.

As we explored in workshops 1 and 2, "peace," biblically speaking, is a peace that will endure. That means a peace where the means of livelihood, work, shelter, and ongoing exchange between creatures with and without feathers, and between creatures and God, is mended and being mended. If peace is a fig tree, then justice is one of its main roots. If there is no justice, there will be no peace. If justice and peace do not kiss, there will be no peace for us to be kissed by.

The Sermon on the Mount's guidance for being kissed by and kissing peace, to which loving one's enemies is so integral, is, not surprisingly, also about labouring for just relationships and labouring in a spirit of freedom that the trust in God-in-Christ brings.

When Christ speaks of being struck on the right cheek, he speaks of the ordinary experience of the poor, the menial workers and others in a subservient social position. Such hitting would be done with the superior's right hand. It would be the right hand, since touching others, even inferiors, with the left hand, the hand associated with toilet tasks and other "dirty" work, was strictly prohibited by religious injunctions and punishments. Hitting would be done with right hand and, as Jesus suggests, on the right cheek. For the would-be superior person, slapping the inferior with the back of the hand would further indicate the recipient's unequal position. The term, "I'll give you the back of my hand," contains the dual meanings found here of not only threat but insult as well. The back of the hand is reserved for inferiors. The palm of the hand or the fist is an acknowledgement of equality, even when it implies a threat.

Now imagine what turning the other cheek does. On the surface it is an invitation to hit again. The slapping superior can't complain about that. However, as acting it out shows, to slap the left cheek with the back of the right hand would require a most awkward and comical stroke and a very undignified position. Yet, to refrain from hitting again raises doubts about the correctness of hitting the first time. Further, to hit the left cheek with the right hand and maintain a dignified appearance requires using the fist or palm, which implies an acknowledgement of the supposed "inferior's" equality.

When the victim neither fights nor flees but turns the other cheek, the situation is no longer dictated by the privileged person. The victim has broken the common pattern of either wilting, or, more rarely, striking back. The latter was suicidal for people from the lower classes, given the unjust court system.

The situation is no longer defined by violence solidified by privilege and submissiveness. The humiliated one raises the small flag of his or her humanity and dignity. The violent one is confronted with the option of stepping back from dominating behaviour and meeting the victim as a person. A more just relationship is seen as a possibility. Of course, there is risk in this for the victim, as there is in other behaviour options. However, there is also the blessing in the gift of one's own ability to respond with imagination and strength. There is the gift of addressing the other as a person of conscience.

Jesus illustrated other creative responses to injustice that make "peace" impossible. We will consider one more illustration.

Jesus again draws on the experience of those made into the least, the poor. "If someone sues you for your cloak give him your undergarment as well." The cloak was the outer garment, the last thing a person without land, house, or property had to offer in pledge for a loan. In scripture, several mentions and rules are made requiring this not uncommon practice: Exodus 22:25-27; Deuteronomy 24:10-13, 17; Amos 2:7-8.

It was just as foolhardy for a debtor from the lowest class to expect justice from the court system as it was for a poor person to strike back at a "respectable" assailant. This reality underlies Christ's and St. Paul's warnings about putting yourself into the hands of the authorities who maintain "law and order." The "legal" execution of Christ and Paul became a further reminder to find ways of settling outside the judicial system.

Jesus suggests a mischievous way of calling for justice if taken to court with their last item to pawn – their cloak or coat. When in court your cloak is demanded, Jesus advises that you give them your underwear as well. This dramatic action says, "You would be so cruel as to take the last garment that shelters me from the weather, you may as well take the rest." There stands the creditor with the law firmly in one hand and the poor person's underwear in the other.

The routine patterns of cruelty that seem to be legal, acceptable, and God-blessed, are disrupted. Jesus offers a disturbing invitation to move in a more just direction. As we have seen before, it is not the situation that offers hope; it is the disadvantaged who, encouraged by a particular sense of "God-with-us," let hope peek through their sorrow.

This suggestion of Jesus echoes his upsetting of the businesses at the temple entrance. Think also of the symbolic actions of Moses and the Prophets; like Ezekiel who knocked a hole in the city wall, and Jeremiah who went about wearing an oxen yoke. These acts anticipate the non-violent resistance to violence and injustice in evidence from the time of the early church to the present day.

(90 min.)

Activity 2

Following the presentation, the group should have an opportunity to ask questions. Once people feel they understand the interpretation presented, the process should proceed.

However, other questions may well arise: Is the confrontation of enemies really "loving"? Does this strategy actually work? Is determining whether or not something works the only way of evaluating our actions? What do we mean by "working"? While such thoughtful questions may arise, ask the group to hold them until you have had time to explore the meaning of this interpretation further.

Participants should turn to the following list of non-violent actions designed to affect the conscience of those they address. Most are self-explanatory. If any actions are not clear, the small-group time may yield an explanation. As each individual goes through the list, they should just skip over, for now, whatever puzzles them.

The first task will be for individuals to choose one action that particularly strikes them. Then they should be asked to imagine a situation in which it might be employed.

The second task is to form into groups of four and tell one another your choice and decide which one to role-play as a group. Once the role-plays have been prepared and performed, the particularly important job of "de-roling" follows.

In de-roling, many earlier as well as new questions will arise and be addressed. What thoughts and feelings arise as we non-violently confront oppression to reveal how many-layered it is? Our reactions reveal the different levels at which non-violence works, and the reason it may not "work" in every sense, or at every level. The question "What thoughts and feelings did you have as you played your role?" allows the de-roling process to begin.

It is important that people allow each other to share thoughts and feelings without being challenged or made to defend them. Once everyone has been able to speak of their experience, the atmosphere will be conducive to an exploration of people's remaining questions.

This list is a selection from the 198 methods of non-violent action in Gene Sharp, *The Politics of Nonviolent Action*, Boston: Porter Sargent Publishers, 11 Beacon Street, Boston, MA 02108.

The Methods of Nonviolent Protest and Persuasion

Formal Statements
1. Public speeches
2. Letters of opposition or support
3. Declarations by organizations and institutions
4. Signed public statements

Communications with a Wider Audience
1. Slogans, caricatures and symbols
2. Banners, posters and displayed communications
3. Records, radio and television
4. Sky writing and earthwriting

Group Representations
1. Deputations
2. Mock awards

Workshop 5

3. Picketing
4. Mock elections

Symbolic Public Acts
1. Displays of flags and symbolic colors
2. Wearing of symbols
3. Prayer and worship
4. Delivering symbolic objects
5. Protest disrobings
6. Destruction of own property
7. Symbolic lights
8. Displays of portraits
9. New signs and names
10. Symbolic reclamations

Pressure on Individuals
1. "Haunting" officials
2. Taunting officals
3. Vigils

Drama and Music
1. Humorous skits and pranks
2. Performances of plays and music
3. Singing

Processions
1. Marches
2. Parades
3. Religious processions
4. Pilgrimages

Honoring the Dead
1. Political mourning
2. Mock funerals
3. Demonstrative funerals
4. Homage at burial places

Public Assemblies
1. Assemblies of protest or support
2. Teach-ins

Withdrawal and Renunciation
1. Walk-outs
2. Silence
3. Renouncing honors
4. Turning one's back

Ostracism of Persons
1. Selective social boycott
2. Lysistratic nonaction

Noncooperation with Social Events, Customs and Institutions
1. Suspension of social and sports activities
2. Social disobedience
3. Withdrawal from social institutions

Withdrawal from the Social System
1. Total personal noncooperation
2. Collective disappearance
3. Protest emigration

Action by Consumers
1. Nonconsumption of boycotted goods
2. Policy of austerity

Action by Holders of Financial Resources
1. Withdrawal of bank deposits
2. Refusal to pay debts or interest
3. Refusal of a government's money

Action by Governments
1. Domestic embargo
2. Blacklisting of traders
3. International sellers' embargo
4. International buyers' embargo
5. International trade embargo

Symbolic Strikes
1. Protest strike
2. Quickie walkout (lightning strike)

Rejection of Authority
1. Withholding or withdrawal of allegiance
2. Literature and speeches advocating resistance

Citizens' Noncooperation with Government
1. Boycott of legislative bodies
2. Boycott of elections
3. Boycott of government-supported organizations
4. Removal of own signs and placemarks
5. Refusal to accept appointed officials

Citizens' Alternatives to Obedience
1. Reluctant and slow compliance
2. Nonobedience in absence of direct supervision
3. Sitdown

4. Hiding, escape and false identities
5. Civil disobedience of "illegitimate" laws

Psychological Intervention
1. Self-exposure to the elements
2. The fast
3. Reverse trial
4. Nonviolent harassment

Physical Intervention
1. Sit-in
2. Stand-in
3. Ride-in
4. Pray-in
5. Nonviolent air raids
6. Nonviolent invasion
7. Nonviolent obstruction
8. Nonviolent occupation

Social Intervention
1. Overloading of facilities
2. Stall-in
3. Guerrilla theater
4. Alternative social institutions

Further questions that may emerge include:

- *"What in your thoughts and emotions resists engaging in such confrontational action?"*

- *"What in your thoughts and feelings encourages such action?"*

Other questions may be addressed, such as:

- *"What is the psychology or mentality that underlies our differing reactions to an oppressive enemy?"*

To react with violence, timidity, or non-violent resistance says something about our view of others and of ourselves. They each say something about our theology. What do they say?

Activity 3
For next week's session, ask everyone to bring a cartoon that makes them laugh.

PART C

(25 min.)

Worship

1. Words of Gathering:

*Come, let us be knit together
into a banner, raised
in praise, to God in Christ,
who spins us, turns us
"little hearts" and "fraidy cheeks,"
that we may seek
justice kissing peace.*

2. Let us pray:

*Thou God, Thou Holy, Thou Mystery.
Plain as bread.
Pained as the Breadman broken, Christ.
With I.O.U.'s of love, we come
hoping against hope you'll never collect.
Bisected by doubts and spirit-sweetened dreams.
With fears and confusions, we come.
These are the gifts we bring,
which we open before you now
in the murmurings of our hearts.
Hear our hearts' whispers, we pray . . .
(time of silence)
We come so far and no farther
unless Thou, Sister Spirit spirit us
hold us, teach us divine foolishness.
Overcoming our cleverest calculations.
Thou, God. Thou, Christ. Thou, Spirit.*

Amen.

3. *This is a reading from Paul's letter to the church at the great commercial port city of Corinth, a church torn by contending factions. Reconciliation between feuding groups was difficult because self-inflating religionists, boasters, and braggarts commanded the stage. Against this tendency, Paul, in the following passage, points to the humble Christ who sought out not the proud or those who knew how to "make it;" not the clever or the worldly wise. To those with "know how," Christ was a fool. This, Paul reminds his listeners, is who we follow. Read 1 Corinthians 1:21-31.*

4. Symbolic action and refrain:

With a few pieces of red grease-paint or lipstick ask everyone to take turns marking the palms of their neighbour. This mark will represent

Workshop 5

the wounds in the hands of Christ who loved the world in all its enmity. This is followed by a period of silence before inviting everyone to join in the following refrain, three times (once in normal volume, once loudly, and once softly).

Refrain:

> *With the redness*
> *we are reminded of the wounds*
> *of neighbour peoples and neighbour nations*
> *of the wounds of God*
> *suffered in Jesus Christ,*
> *crucified and risen.*

Each person is then asked to mark the nose of their neighbour and to their neighbour, repeat three times (once in normal volume, once loudly, and once softly):

You have a red nose like me,
a fool clown.
May you and I
be given the heart and mind
of fools in Christ.

5. Song: "Your Feet Will Not Stumble."

6. Benediction:

Go in the blessed unrest of Christ's love
and good company. Amen.

Your Feet Will Not Stumble

Words & Music by Ian Macdonald

Your feet will not stum-ble, your strength will be re-newed; God's ea-gle wings will lift your soul, and love will be your food. 1. Lis-ten to the ev-'ning rains, watch the dew rise with the dawn. Walk for peace down the crow-ded streets, and walk when the crowds have gone. Don't keep your heart from break-ing, there are tides to ev-'ry sea. Find the prom-is-es that can keep you, sing the songs that set you free. And your

© Common Cup Company, Inc., 271 Queenston Street, Winnipeg, Manitoba R3N 0W9.
Used by permission.

Your Feet Will Not Stumble/cont.

2. Stand beside the beds of sorrow,
   Honour lives that come and go.
   Words will come to ease your pain,
   As the dark nights ebb and flow.
   God's promise is a blessing,
   Whispered low and whispered long,
   The sun will bring the morning light,
   Your life is in God's dawn. And your...
   (Chorus)

3. Listen to your laughter,
   As it mingles with your tears,
   Wherever you're happy,
   Wherever you have tears.
   For God's own Joy is rising,
   Like an ev'ning tide,
   Lifting off the faded scars,
   Your years have tried to hide. And your...
   (Chorus)

4. Listen to your anger,
   Where justice is denied.
   Listen to the cries of those
   Whose hope life over-rides.
   Remember them in deeds and prayers,
   In the watches of the night.
   Keep creation turning round again,
   'Till the world turns out right. And your...
   (Chorus)

Musings

When I speak to my creator,
my God, I speak from somewhere within my heart.
It is something very hard to describe –
only that it is very near to some deep place within.
Always when I pray, I pray in my own language
because this is how I feel I may speak most closely to God.
It is very deeply personal.
When the minister asked me to pray during the service
I stood in the aisle,
and, closing my eyes, lifted my heart in prayer.
As I began, someone beside me said,
"Speak English – I don't understand a word you're saying."
I think you would say I was stunned in a way.
I tried as I stood there to think of what I might say,
how I might explain. Then I said,
"I am sorry if it is upsetting for you,
I do not mean to upset you. But you see –
it is not you I am speaking to,
it is my Lord I am speaking to

and I think God will understand the words of my heart."

I did not know what else to say,
but I was very hurt.

– *Elder Gladys Taylor*

Jesus with dance masks of lion and lamb

> I used to be a peaceful duck, enjoying grasses and green shoots and hoping that someday cousin Wolf would give up his diet of flesh of rabbit, partridge and... duck.

> Cousin Wolf would tell me that we are all wolves under the skin. I used to argue, then I began thinking, maybe he's right.

> So I tried it. I ate a rabbit when she was sleeping and a partridge with a broken wing.

> I'm still a peaceful duck. It's just that now I'm teaching my duckling to kill woodchucks and eat flesh. But today he asked, "What does old duck taste like?"

One of the most common arguments peacemakers face is that aggression is best discouraged by threatening equal or greater aggression. It is the belief that we deter by a readiness to *inter*.

The assumption is that the main cause of violent conflict or war preparations is simply the failure of the aggressor to clearly calculate the cost of aggression. When we respond with threats and intimidation, the aggressor (who we can assume is "them" and not "us") is expected to become more "reasonable" and clear-headed about the consequences of his actions.

Deterrence implies a great trust, if not faith, in the power of intimidation and the power to kill. Deterrence places its trust in death and the technologies of death. What may at very best "work" on rare occasions has become the ruling creed. The reduction of complex economic, religious, and political differences to a strictly military problem makes more profound analysis or response unlikely. Deterrence discounts what leads up to violent conflict. It is short-sighted about "solutions." Nevertheless, it persists as an argument that must be dealt with.

WORKSHOP 6

"Don't make me laugh!": satire as bitter medicine.

Satire is well described in George Orwell's opinion of jokes. Their "aim" he says, "is not to degrade the human being but to remind him that he is already degraded." People who are satirized need a reminder because they either forget that they are already degraded, or they pretend that there is nothing to forget. Usually the degradation is simply hidden by the hypocrite who covers it over with prevailing religious or political cliché or jargon. Nevertheless, such situations need to be uncovered and exposed so that they can be confronted.

The satirical exposure of degradation and cruelty is often misunderstood. The ridiculing finger that points at cruelty can itself be seen as cruel. For instance, in Matthew 23, when Jesus points out the injustices of the scribes and the Pharisees, which they dress up with "Lord, Lord" language, Jesus himself may be seen as cruel. Some satire – that of the prophets, Jesus, as well as later satirists who follow – is bitter medicine. However, it is only occasional medicine, reserved for those with power over others; that is, for those whose behaviour affects the undefended lives of many innocent people.

Satire helps to prevent the degradation of the weak by the powerful. This workshop is designed to enrich our understanding of satire's place in helping us to limp toward God's peaceable commonwealth.

Objectives:

- To learn to see through the rhetoric and falsehood that surround militarism and injustice.
- To achieve this insight through the vehicle of satire as practiced by Jesus, and as found in a sampling of satirical cartoons.

PART A

(6 min.)

Activity 1

Everyone is invited to take a moment to identify their favourite comic character from comic strips, television programs, or movies.

After naming a favourite character, people are asked to pair off and share: (1) the reason he or she finds that character funny and,
(2) the favourite cartoon that they selected from the week's reading.

(25 min.)

Activity 2

Introductory remarks: *Comedy has a lot to do with pleasing contradictions. We expect one thing and are pleasantly surprised by another. The arrogant traffic meter officer strutting down the street with his nose in the sky rejoins the earthy clay because of an unseen banana peel. There is a contradiction between his strutting pride and his landing buttocks; between his apparent arrogance and his regained humility.*

Comedy is about pleasing contradictions in events, behaviour, character, or ideas. But of course, the contradictions may not be pleasing to everyone. Whether they are pleasing to you depends on where you stand in relation to them. It all depends on your viewpoint, which is not generally yours alone; it is a view you share with your group or community. In short, we could say that comedy is a pleasing contradiction apparent to those whose perspective allows them to see more pleasure than pain in the situation.

With these few thoughts in mind, let's take two of the cartoons brought in and see if we, as a group, can describe their effect using some of the elements of comedy just mentioned. What is the contradiction in the cartoon? Is it in images or words? Who might not find this funny? Who might find it very funny? Why?

PART B

(37 min.)

Activity 1

Introductory remarks: *Jesus often used comic devices in his teaching and preaching, as did his forerunners, the prophets. In Matthew 13, for example, Jesus describes the most mysterious of gifts, the heavenly kingdom of God, using the most mundane articles: a pinch of yeast, a midget seed of mustard. His lovingly comical associations of the high God are no less lowly, as in the unjust judge of Luke (18: 1-8). God listens like the unjust judge, only more so. These humorous contradictions present what is high as lowly, and what is lowly as created in the image of the Highest. This is "laughter with" more than "laughter at."*

Sometimes Jesus calls forth "laughter at," derisive laughter. Like the prophets, he corrects with harsher comedy, or satire. His satire contains anger at the powerful for their denial of God's graciousness. Jesus never uses satire against the poor. He uses it often against the self-serving religion of the middle and upper classes, represented by the scribes and Pharisees.

Jesus' satire is directed at idolatry and false authority – religious, political, or military. Idolatry and false authority cause the people to be serious about the wrong things. Satirical comedy in scripture is based upon a seriousness about God's peace, justice, and mercy for all of creation. From that standpoint, it works at exposing or seeing through all kinds of false piety.

In pairs, examine Matthew 23: 23-28.

- *What does Jesus ridicule in each verse?*
- *What images does he use for each satirical contradiction?*

After quickly noting the lessons from Jesus' satires, consider, as a group, who among Jesus' listeners might find these satirical pinches funny. Who would not find them funny? Why?

PART C

(36 min.)

Activity 1

Introduction to the cluster of drawings satirizing different aspects of militarism:

We are perhaps accustomed to comic drawings that are immediately understood. Some of your collection are like that, while others may need pondering. If a drawing's comedy is not immediate, begin by naming the images you see in the drawing and in the caption. The way in which they are arranged one against the other should help the ideas unfold.

The task moves from individual work to work in pairs.

Go through the drawings a couple of times. Pick the one that you find the most striking. Try to identify the comic contradictions or conflicts that it exposes. What devices are used to make the cartoon work: images, wording, and so on?

Share your chosen drawing with your partner. Explore them together and then explore the other drawings that strike you. What ideas or false authorities do they expose?

In the total group have each pair share one cartoon they found striking and explain why.

PART D

(25 min.)

Worship

1. Words of Gathering:

Come let us be gathered in worship of the God who laughs the mighty from the heights and leaves banana skins before our pride, the God for whom whales and giants are toys and the noise of our praise can be song.

Workshop 6

2. Let us join in a roundabout confession, a litany that mocks excuses for unfaithfulness:

Leader: If only we had wings like Noah's dove . . .

People: (repeated response)
> **Then, our hearts would be**
> **Hot, not cold, for God's mercy**
> **Making and shaping our day**

Leader: If we had a jawbone like Samson's donkey

People: (repeated response)

Leader: If we saw a bush aburning like Moses

People: (repeated response)

Leader: If only we had Ruth or Sarah by our side

People: (repeated response)

Leader: If we had a pail like the woman at the well

People: (repeated response)

Leader: If we had a tail like Peter's rooster

People: (repeated response)

Leader: If only we saw Easter rise with Magdalen's eyes

People: (repeated response)

Leader and People: O Gracious God, help us laugh our sombre and silly excuses away. Please spirit our hearts with courage and grant us the strength to weep and the wisdom that weeping brings. In the name of Christ, our compassionate companion. Amen.

3. Read Matthew 23:37-39.

In Matthew 23, following Jesus' comic pinches of the scribes and Pharisees, there is an apparent shift in Jesus' mood from anger to sadness over the frustrating blindness of the Holy City, which the scribes and Pharisees see themselves as protecting. Sorrowfully, Jesus speaks of himself as a mother hen. This mood is only seemingly unrelated to the satire that went before, which, like satire generally, contains unspoken sadness. In this passage Jesus draws out the sadness and speaks it. Take a moment to go through the cartoons you focussed on, and identify what about the situation in each makes you sad.

4. Bidding Prayer:

O Holy God of Mystery and Mercy, of evening and morning, and night and night's turning to day. Blessed be your name. We come to you in need of your spirit, and we come with offerings of pennies, and buttons, and worn shirts of sorrow and sadness. Hear us as we speak to you of our sadness. (Period of spoken or silent prayer.) If our shirts of sorrow are still to be worn awhile, grant us buttons of laughter and fill our pockets with hope. In Christ's name, we ask it. Amen.

5. Song: "Cana Wine."

6. Benediction:

Go now in the blessed unrest of God's spirit that yearns for the earth's mending. Amen.

Cana Wine

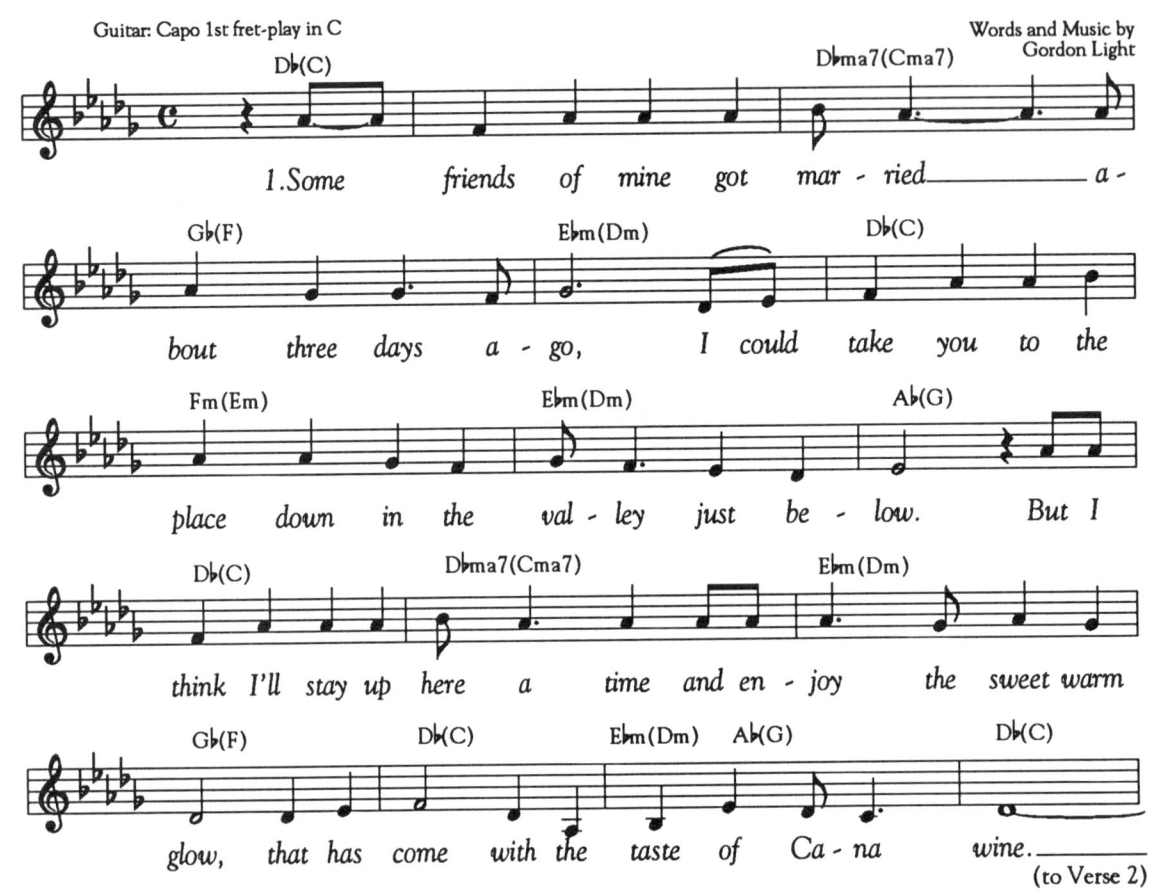

Guitar: Capo 1st fret-play in C

Words and Music by Gordon Light

1. Some friends of mine got married about three days ago, I could take you to the place down in the valley just below. But I think I'll stay up here a time and enjoy the sweet warm glow, that has come with the taste of Cana wine.
(to Verse 2)

2. It was just a simple wedding feast,
   You know the kind I mean,
   Holding hands, holding hearts,
   And holding fast to all their dreams.
   But somehow I got the feeling
   It was more than first it seemed,
   Must have been from the taste of Cana wine.
   (Chorus)

3. I didn't have that much to drink,
   But I never felt so tall,
   The wine was finding empty holes
   I hadn't known at all.
   It touched the deepest hurts in me,
   'Till it found and filled my soul.
   Never tasted the like of Cana wine.
   (Chorus)

4. That marriage down in Cana,
   Brought new life to my friends,
   I bless them and I wish them all
   The fullness life can bring.
   But a new life's rising in me too,
   Like an overflowing stream,
   And it comes from the taste of Cana wine.
   (Chorus)

© Common Cup Company, Inc., 271 Queenston Street, Winnipeg, Manitoba R3N 0W9.
Used by permission.

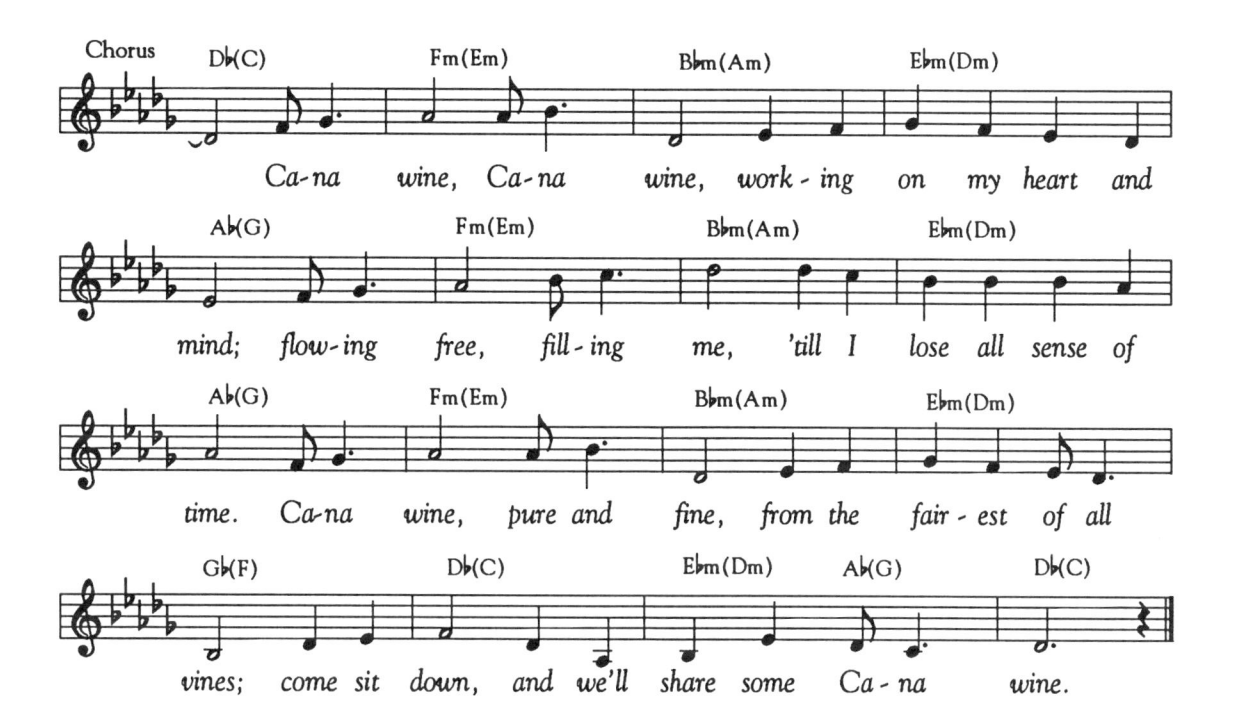

Cana Wine/cont.

Chorus

Ca-na wine, Ca-na wine, work-ing on my heart and mind; flow-ing free, fill-ing me, 'till I lose all sense of time. Ca-na wine, pure and fine, from the fair-est of all vines; come sit down, and we'll share some Ca-na wine.

| Panel 1 | When I first got my dog, he kept jumping up. I clouted him. He stopped jumping up. |

| Panel 2 | The dog got into barking. A smack on the nose and he stopped barking. |

| Panel 3 | Last night, he snored. I bit his ear. He stopped snoring — and bit off my tail! |

| Panel 4 | Thats the trouble with dogs — they are prone to violence. |

Workshop 6

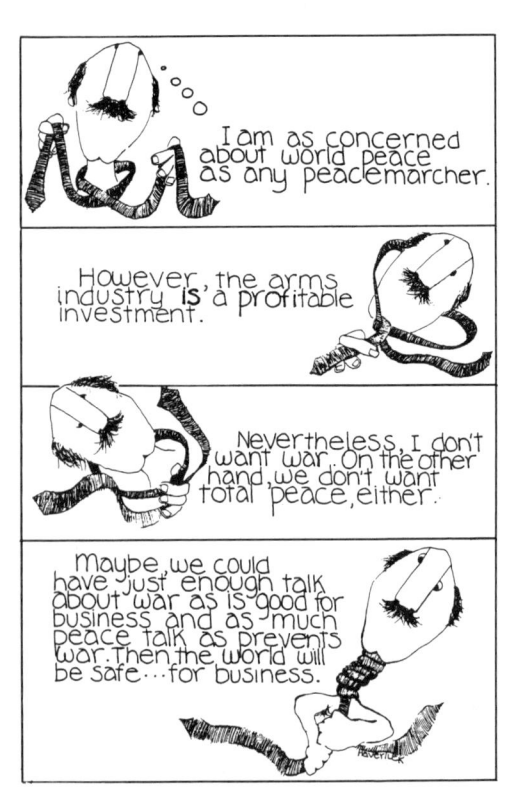

> I am as concerned about world peace as any peacemarcher.
>
> However, the arms industry *is* a profitable investment.
>
> Nevertheless, I don't want war. On the other hand, we don't want total peace, either.
>
> Maybe we could have just enough talk about war as is good for business and as much peace talk as prevents war. Then the world will be safe... for business.

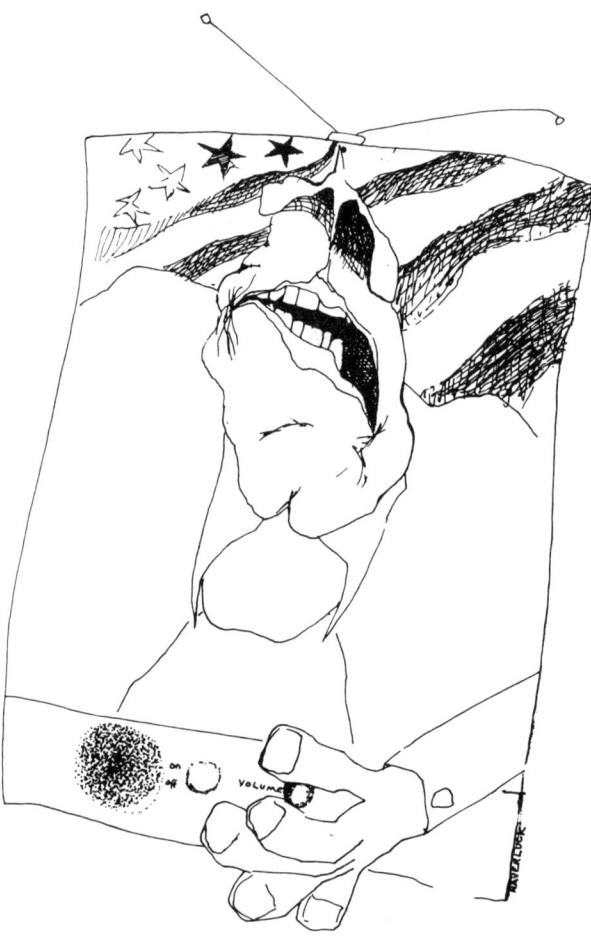

There are commies out there claiming Jesus says "love your enemies". That all rests on a typing error. He never said that. He said "Love your Aunt Emmie!" Now I don't have an Aunt Emmie. So that doesn't apply. As for — "Sell all you have to the poor!" I tried that. They weren't buying.

Love Your Enemies

See my finger
See my thumb
see my missiles
you'd better run.

We would have a lot less complaining and whining in this country if everyone were white like me. Of course that's impossible, since most people are pink... with red spotty bits on their bums.

Workshop 6

Of course, everybody wants peace. And we are glad to play a little part.

Let's be frank. If there weren't any Russians, we'd have to invent them!

Political? Worldly nonsense! These nails are spiritual. The cross is just a cloud and Pilate is your Aunt Sally.

76　　　　　Love Your Enemies

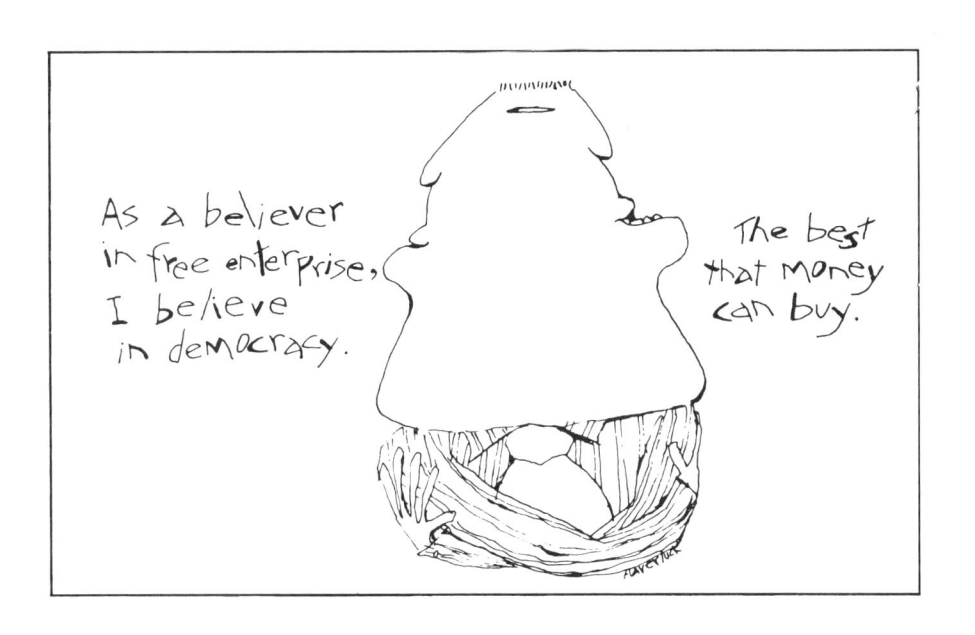

"As a believer in free enterprise, I believe in democracy. The best that money can buy."

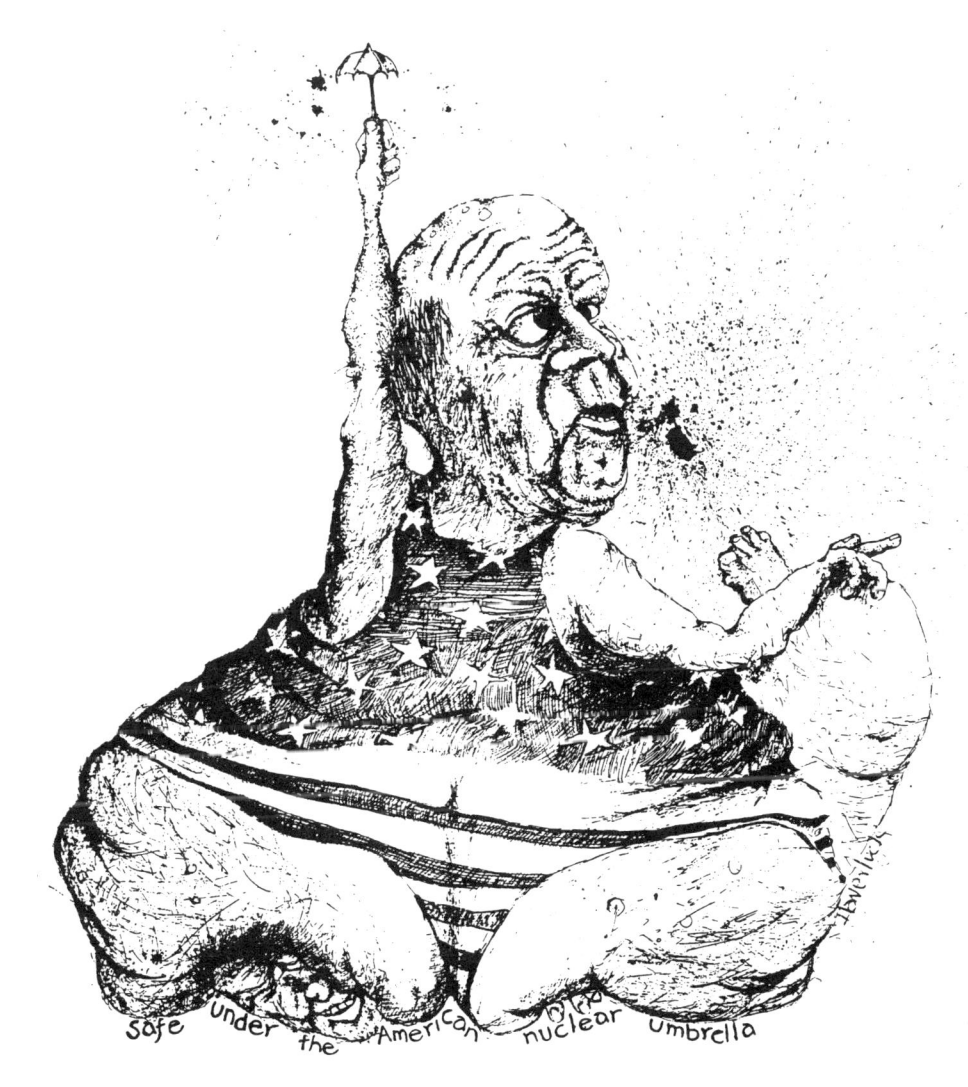

safe under the American nuclear umbrella

Workshop 6

Musings

An Invitation to Laugh

Satire is the comedy Jesus and scripture use to ridicule the refusals of God's gracious Commonwealth. Recall the satirical portrayals of those who refuse to be taken in by the divine hospitality of the great feast (Luke 14, Matt. 22). Satire with its "laughter at" is found throughout scripture and also serves to unmask the sincere smiles and sneers on the faces of the arrogant authorities.

How can a modern-day artist depict refusals of grace like those satirized by Jesus and the prophets? Where is religiosity used to evade faithfulness to the God of justice and mercy? Where is brutality mystified with the language of virtue and the symbols of honour? It was not any or every contradiction between ideal and practice that was of concern to the biblical satirists. The contradictions and incongruities of special interest were ones where power over others was concentrated. Concentrations of economic and military might, and the power to shape vision and values, needed and still needs satire.

Those whose security is chained to injustice, to false limits, will experience much of what the prophets find laughable as "not funny." So, too, Jesus' comic jibes will be seen as not funny to the oppressive class of the new Pharisees and Sadducees. For Jesus' satires show little regard for either their good intentions or their bits of truth. It is important for us as middle-class Canadians (who are safe as houses … built on sand) to be open to laughter which is directed at us. Such laughter will feel like pinches meant for our correction. But if we will not be corrected by laughter, we will be awakened by much harsher things.

We will never all agree – until resurrection day – on what we can laugh at, or whom we laugh with. To those made the least, humour and satire consoles and makes clear and corrects. Such laughter is the stuff of a daydream:

Once, when times were very troubled and injustice ruled, a group of creatures gathered before God and prayed. For the peaceable commonwealth, they prayed. To them God spoke, saying, "Be of good spirit, justice and mercy will come and will kiss." "We believe this," the people replied. "But until then, could we have something on loan?" God smiled. "Yes." And gave them – laughter. God did this lest the holy name be spoken in vain.

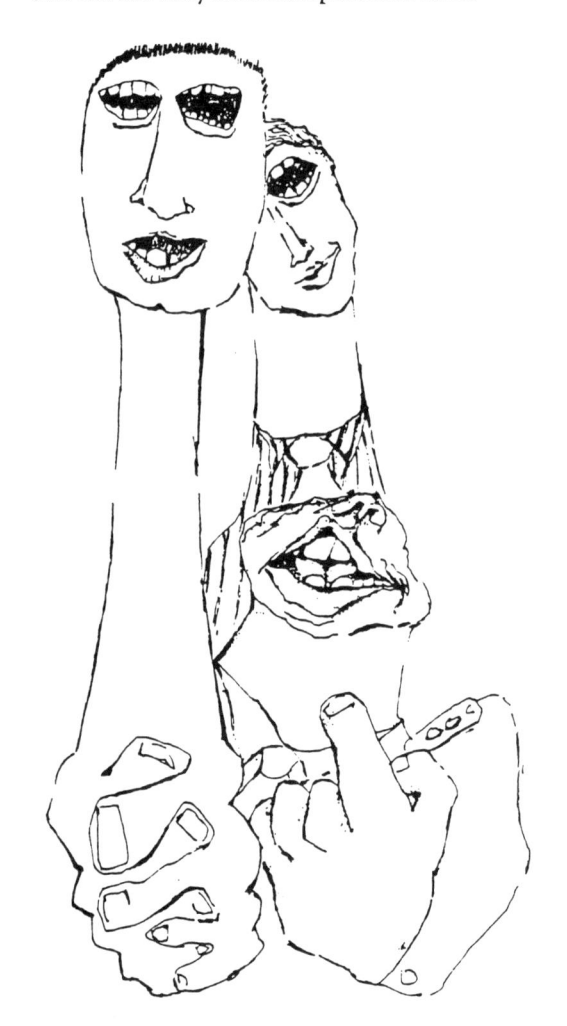

Government negotiators at Oka

Angel re-inflating a deflated prophet

Lord of all creation, scorner of pharoahs and kings, do you and your angels make mock of us and sing satires of our follies? Bedazzled and captivated by threats and promises, we follow our fears most carefully but host your Spirit rarely. Cross-purposed, cross-eyed and straight-faced, we feed on fruits not of your kingdom. Refusing to be drawn by your love, or shamed and tamed as the laughing-stock of heaven, we pray, our God, do not leave us to become the praiseworthies of hell. Let us begin to fear and hear your scorning laughter rather than the voices of the protectors of worldly treasures. We pray, Lord, that in hearing we will be healed enough to hurry after your love beyond measure. Amen.

– from *Keep Awake With Me*

WORKSHOP 7

No more bucks for the Bang: the economic appeals of militarism.

Many of us recognize fears about economic security working on us from time to time. In national and regional spheres, this fear about security also exists; particularly over the loss of apparent economic benefits that result from military industries. Therefore, even while we wish for a world at peace, there is support for military research, industry, and bases.

A pressing task for us is the recognition of a conflict within ourselves as a nation, as a city, and as individuals. We want peace, but not the kind of economics that make for peace. We want the kind of economy that makes for war; without the war, of course.

Given the money surrounding things military, especially the huge profits from military industries, we cannot ignore the military industrial partnerships' resistance to reductions in military spending. Predictably, the defense of this warfare state is mixed with the most elevated religious and political rhetoric. Identifying military-economic motivations and imagining alternative industries become the tasks of peacemaking communities.

In this workshop we want to engage the pervasive economic appeal of the military industry. We will also identify some of the tasks and resources we have for untangling economics and militarism.

Objectives:

- To help folks re-affirm that their security rests in Christ and Christ's body rather than in the "power" of financial security.
- To help us see through the marriage of money and power; its influence on economics, politics, and militarism.
- To reveal the idolatry in our respect for money.

PART A

(4 min.)

Activity 1 – Warm Up
(To move us toward writing some group rhymes.)

I am going to ask "Mary" to say a word, any word: for example, "free." The next person says any word that rhymes: for example, "tea," and we continue rhyming. If someone gets stuck, we will wait a moment, after which coaching will be acceptable. We will have three rounds with a different word and starter each time.

(8 min.)

Activity 2
This time we will go around trying to make a rhyme using simple phrases rather than just one word: for example, "The moose is loose / and so is the goose / Quick Toulouse, the goose." It might not be great, but it will be our own. We will have two or three rounds.

PART B

(3 min.)

Activity 1 – Exercise
(To imagine following Christ the peacemaker.)

In this exercise we will explore how following Christ the peacemaker means resisting the seductive appeals of financial security. We will do this by composing a litany which affirms that God alone is our security, and that other claims are false and lead us into the support of policies of violence and war.

Our subject is serious. The litany we write in our makeshift poetry will be playful because, as Christians, we take only God's authority seriously. We take worldly powers lightly. We refuse to let the powers of this world pretend to have the authority of God.

To keep our litany focussed and our task manageable, we are given a chorus of rough poetry. We will write the verses. The chorus goes:

Our security is not in money or might;
Their promising kisses, their terrifying bite.
No I ain't money's boy
And I ain't muscles' girl
I'm a free child of God
Creature of God's world.

In a few minutes we will put together a verse based on a passage from the book End the Arms Race: Fund Human Needs. *However, before that and in preparation for that, we have two things to ponder. The first is an overview of scripture's repeated warning against seeking financial security, mammon, or money. The second is an introduction to the passage we are going to put into rough verse.*

(7 min.)

Activity 2
One freedom that is a gift of following Christ is the freedom from obsessions about financial security. Consider Zacchaeus, who proves his conversion by immediately sharing his property with the poor (Luke 19:8). Consider the

Workshop 7

early church in Jerusalem, whose members sold their possessions and distributed the money among the poor. In the needs of the poor they saw Christ Jesus' need (Acts 4:32-35). Living simply, without many possessions, the early church was more capable of avoiding the trap that accumulation, maintenance, and protection of possessions creates.

Recall Jesus' encounter with the rich young ruler, who was generous and religious. Jesus agreed to save him from the poverty of soul that his riches inevitably caused. "Sell all you have, give the money to the poor, and come and follow me" (Luke 18:22). Jesus tried to wean him from his golden soother and have him experience the freedom of Christ's company instead. His company is always "instead" of the gold comforter. "You cannot serve both God and Mammon, God and financial security," says Jesus.

Living in the good company of Christ provides a security that is obviously not what our society understands as security; that is, military or economic security. And we know this, half-heartedly. But to know it heartily means seeking and being content with daily bread that is in keeping with God's promised kingdom, with God's commonwealth. Knowing it fully means being able to detect the deadly workings of economic interests underneath the smiles, the religious explanations, and the patriotic jargon. It means seeing the attraction of financial security as the gospel predominantly sees it: not as neutral, but as a constant temptation. Jesus' parables and satires (Luke 12:13-21, 14:28-33; Matt. 23:16-26) reveal the foolishness of worldly security. The dangerous and deadly aspects of money pervade the whole biblical drama.

Near the axis of the biblical drama, Jesus is bought and sold for slaughter at the price of thirty pieces of silver. The crucifixion occurs because of Jesus' ongoing confrontations with the "Lord, Lord"-talking Pharisees who are secret lovers of money, according to the Gospel of Luke (16:9-15). The crucifixion is also an outcome of Jesus' overthrowing the tables of the Jerusalem moneychangers at the temple (Mark 11:15-19). Those lovers of financial security are part of the host of powers whose religious, political, and military arms are synonymous with the push for more and more worldly security. St. John uncovers such machinations in one of scripture's closing scenes (Rev. 18).

St. John draws the picture of an economic empire which appears to be specifically Roman, but which reveals a good deal about the corpses upon which all economic empires are built. The empire's ability to buy and sell the luxuries of every nation insures the loyalty of the rich and powerful. This "number one" nation is impressive if the eyes are fixed exclusively on its commercial splendours. St. John shifts our eyes to the murdered prophets and saints of the God of Love and Justice and says that the economic empire is responsible for "all the blood that was ever shed on the earth" (18:24).

Allowing for a little exaggeration, the wisdom of this revelation remains.

In conclusion, we should remember that Christ's good company offers freedom amidst these powers, pressures, and enticements. And it is this freedom that allows us to see how violence is used constantly to maintain the monied interests.

Activity 3

(10 min.)

With this in mind we turn to a little story in the book of Acts:

Time: *a few years after the death and resurrection of Christ.*

Place: *Phillipi in present-day Turkey. (At that time a thriving Roman commercial city.)*

Characters: *Paul and Silas.*

Occasion: *Paul's return to the city to help strengthen the Phillipi church.*

Story: *from Acts 16:16-23 (read once aloud). Did you notice Paul's almost comical motivation for healing the slave girl?*

Before we read this passage again, I ask a further question: "What appeals are used to set the crowd and the magistrates against Paul and Silas?" (Not incidentally, Paul's healing of the slave girl has just put the businessmen out of business.)

Activity 4

(30 min.)

Let's hear the story again, and clarify the above question before we rewrite the story in verse.

Our objective is only to clarify the *details* of the story. Invite discussion of the interpretation of the story only when the group is choosing lines for their own version. The objective of the litany-writing exercise is to playfully retell the incident in the group's own words. In so doing, they see how financial powers disguise their true interests in hypocritical language that hides the injustice of the situation.

Does scripture not warn us that injustice is often "dressed up" in what is "legal" and "orderly?" Our idea is to let such thoughts emerge through the process of verse-writing. So move as quickly as possible to asking for suggestions for one or two starting lines. Write them on separate sheets so that everyone can see. As you carry on with the writing, suitable interpretations will emerge. Remember you need not rhyme the end of every line. No need to worry about poetic greatness here. Have fun together.

If you have trouble with one starting line, try another, and if there is time, do two versions. When finished, read the litany aloud (loudly) together. You will have the proposed chorus already pasted up. Invite quick comments on the verse: "What do you like in it? Is there anything essential that you feel has been left out?" Let these be heard by the whole group, but don't be drawn into a long discussion.

Activity 5

(40 min.)

Divide into pairs or small working groups, depending on your numbers and the language skills of your people. Give them the following excerpt from a speech on Canada's part in the military economic establishment, "Our War Economy and Conversion for Peace" by Bishop Remi J. De Roo, from *End the Arms Race: Fund Human Needs*, ed. Thomas L. Perry & James G. Foulks, West Vancouver, 1986. Ask the groups to read it over twice and then to decide on a section or sections they would like to put into crude rhyme. Remind them to discuss it only until you get basic enough agreement to begin. They will reach agreement or clarify disagreements in the process of writing.

Global War Economy

First, we must recognize that we live in the midst of a "global war economy." Since the Second World War, the United States and the Soviet Union have primarily organized their own national economies (and the economies of many of their satellite countries) around the priorities of escalating military production. As a result, vast resources of capital and technology have been directed toward building a global war economy, not only East and West but also North and South....

Canada's Role

Secondly, we must identify the role that Canada plays in this global war economy. Canada is a member of the Western political alliance through NATO and NORAD. Canada's economy is highly dependent upon that of the United States. The more Canada's economy is tied to that of our powerful neighbour, the more Canada operates as a branch plant of the American military-industrial complex in a high-tech nuclear age.

As a nation-state, Canada has officially rejected the nuclear option. Yet Canada actively participates in the production of nuclear weapon systems. Through the Canadian-American Defence Production Sharing Arrangement, Canadian industries have been directly involved in the production of component parts for nuclear weapon systems, including cruise missiles, Trident submarines, and launchers for the neutron bomb. Canadian scientists and high-tech industries have also been involved in the production of communication systems and related technologies for nuclear weapon systems. Many of these projects for nuclear weapons research are funded in part by the Canadian government under the Defence Industry Production Program.

Canadian territory has also become increasingly important to the United States in the development of nuclear war-fighting strategies. In British Columbia, the coastal waters near Nanoose Bay are probably used for the testing of nuclear warheads as well as for Trident submarine manoeuvres. Parts of Alberta and the Northwest Territories are used for the flight tests of cruise missiles. More importantly, it is highly likely that the Canadian north will play a strategic role in the American "Star Wars" program. As numerous observers have pointed out, the recent renewal of the NORAD agreement, coupled with the decision to rebuild the continental defence system in northern Canada, sets the stage for Canada's involvement in Star Wars and its nuclear war-fighting operations.

At the same time, Canadian arms manufacturers have been actively selling arms to Third World military regimes. Sales include military and police equipment to the Pinochet regime in Chile; equipment and technologies which are probably used for military or police operations in South Africa; and aircraft to the military regime in Honduras. The sales of CANDU nuclear technology to military regimes in South Korea and Argentina also raises serious questions. More recently, a Canadian manufacturing subsidiary supplied armoured vehicles for the new American rapid deployment force, which is expected to be used for military intervention in areas of regional conflict, such as Nicaragua.

In effect, Canada has come to play an increasingly important role in the global war economy, both as a branch plant of the American military economy and as a territorial base for American nuclear strategies. In many ways Canada has become the United States' economic and political satellite.

Moral Disorder
Thirdly, we need to clarify the extent to which the global war economy and Canada's role in it constitute a moral disorder. The global war economy poses a real threat to the future of both humanity and creation itself. This, in turn, presents a fundamental challenge to all our religious traditions and categories of moral judgment. For what is at stake is nothing less than the survival of the human race and the earth itself which God created *good*.

From both a religious and a humanistic standpoint, the fact that billions of dollars are spent every day on military weapons, while millions of people are suffering from poverty and starvation in the world, is a scandal of the highest proportions. Under these conditions, human and material resources are being mobilized for the service of death rather than the source of life. The service of death may be a slow process, as in the case of human starvation or military repression in Third World countries. Or it may be a rapid process, as in the case of a nuclear holocaust. In either case, we are confronted with a profound moral disorder in the values and priorities that govern our global economy.

We Canadians are seriously misled if we act as innocent bystanders in all this. As the United States prepares to "sacrifice arms control on the altar of SDI (strategic defense initiatives)," as Rear Admiral Eugene Carroll expressed it, are we not in some way willing acolytes bowing before the golden idol of military profits? And when public authorities tell Canadian workers in certain regions that they have to choose between jobs in military production or unemployment, is this not a form of inhuman blackmail which must be identified and denounced?"

Economic Conversion

Fourthly, we need to make concerted efforts to develop new and effective strategies for economic conversion in Canada. After all, the very existence of a global war economy implies that national economies become increasingly dependent on military production. Any real strategy for peace in a nuclear age requires industrial conversion from military production priorities to more socially useful forms of production. In effect, economic conversion is essential for addressing the moral disorder of a global war economy in a nuclear age.

(10 min.)

Activity 6

Put up the new verses and read your litany together. Take a moment afterward to invite people to say aloud what pleased or troubled them about the new verses they heard. Ask people to be "economical" with their comments. The purpose is only to share responses, not to discuss or agree about responses. It is enough to state your response and to hear it. I trust that people will mull the ideas over in their own time and not feel that everything needs to be defended.

PART C

(35 min.)

Worship

Space should include a centre-piece with a cross, an offering plate, and a garbage can. The two litanies the group has formulated during the workshop should be posted so that everyone can read them.

1. Words of Gathering:

*Let us be gathered and held
in God's embrace. Trusting
in God's promises. Trusting
in God's Spirit to shape our days.*

2. A reading from Matthew 6:19-21, 24, 25-34; 7:21-27.

3. Let each group read aloud its verse about:
- our military economy and responses, and,
- the story of the girl possessed taken from Acts.

4. Symbolic Action:

The symbolic action to follow will require a two-dollar bill and two loonies for each person. The exercise entails preparing for meditation by taping the bill over the heart, and placing a one-dollar coin over each eye. This money should be the participants' own, so an anticipatory word would be helpful the week before. In any case, you should have spare bills and loonies on hand in case you have to make change or spot someone the cash.

After everyone has their money out and is sitting comfortably, introduce the exercise that may evoke unease. Whether because it is strange, new, emotional, or whatever, this unease is best acknowledged. To name it is to make its occurrence more ordinary, acceptable, and far less disruptive to the individual and the group.

We are all about to join in an exercise which may make you want to laugh a little. While having a comical look to it, our activity is also serious. We are simply going to do, in a literal fashion, what our society does figuratively on a daily basis. Once in that mode, I will to lead you in a short meditation exercise.

Let us begin by each of us carefully taping a two-dollar bill over our heart. Let everyone tape one loony over their neighbour's left eye. Can everyone now get comfortably seated, or lying down? Let us take our remaining loony, grip it in our right hand and place that closed hand over our right eye.

Once you are comfortable, listen for the sound of your own breathing. Take deeper breaths now, and blow out as much old air as you can. Let your breathing become slower and deeper. Let your body loosen and relax.

Workshop 7

Let yourself be aware of the weight of the money over your left eye and feel the tightness of your hand holding money against your right eye. Feel the lightness of the money covering your heart. Is it so light that you can't even feel it there? Question for you to ponder: "How does your concern for financial security for yourself (or your family) block your works of compassion for God's world?"

A second question to ponder: "What changes in your life can you make to enable you (and your family) to work and live more freely for justice and peacemaking?"

In a moment, I'm going to lead you in two actions. The first is an offering of the loonies on your eye and in your hand. In the second, I will invite you to take the two-dollar bill that covers your heart, tear it off, rip it up, and then place it in the garbage can as a sign of our wish for God's help in freeing us from our trust in economic security. We may be resistant to destroying this money. It is a powerful symbol of our society's "true" religion. Think about it in the presence of God, who is discounted by our society's way of life with its religion of economic security and resultant militarism.

5. People are invited to get up and place their offering in the offering plate and then to pray.

O Holy, Holy, Holy, Gracious and Merciful,
Yet lowly as a sculptor, shaping clay and giving it
breath, giving us days. We, your creatures of borrowed
breath, thank you for the gift of breathing awhile.

To our ashes and dust, you are breath.
To chaos, you are creation and creating.
To captivity, you are resurrection and insurrection.
We, your creatures of borrowed breath, thank you.

In our trusting of your mercy, we confess our dis-trust.
We confess that often our hope and trust lie in money
and security and the comforts and privileges they
promise, for our families and for ourselves. Hear
the confession of our hearts as we speak them aloud
or in the silence . . .

To captivity, you are resurrection and insurrection.
To heart-felt confession, you are forgiveness.

We pray for your help, O God, to allow us to be freed
from the machinations of money as was the young woman
possessed.

As we pray for greater faithfulness, hear our prayers,
as we speak them aloud or in the silence of our hearts . . .

*Where we can't see a way, show us ways; where we
are half-hearted, make us hearty – us, and all your
daughters and sons, every one.*

*Let our throwing away of the money that covers
our heart, and let our offerings be to your honour.*

In Christ's name, we seek it. Amen.

At this point the worship leader goes forward, tears up the bill covering his or her own heart, puts it in the garbage, and invites the others to do the same.

6. Song: "Be Thou My Vision."

7. Benediction:

*Go now in peace,
trusting in the mercy
and promises of God and
Jesus Christ, our
companion and our hope.
Amen.*

Following the worship, you should be prepared to remain awhile to discuss people's reactions to the symbolic act of "tearing up good money that could have been spent on something useful." Others may wish to speak of feeling "release" or "freedom" through the symbolic act. Still others may want to explore or simply state that we daily "throw away good money" on unnecessary clothing, fancy foods, adult toys, living space – rather than perform acts which would open ourselves to God.

Be Thou My Vision

Ancient Irish; Ps. 119
Tr. Mary E. Byrne, 1905
Versified by Eleanor H. Hull 1912
Guitar: Capo 1st fret-play in D

SLANE 10.10.9.10
Trad. Irish Melody
Harm. by David Evans, 1927

1. Be thou my vision, the joy of my heart;
Nought be all else to me save that thou art.
Thou my best thought, by day or by night,
Waking or sleeping, thy presence my light.

2. Be thou my wisdom, the lamp to my feet;
Thy word, like honey, to my lips is sweet;
Thou my delight, my joy, thy command;
My dwelling ever, be the palm of thy hand.

3. Riches I heed not, nor seek human praise;
Thou mine inheritance, now and always;
Thou and thou only, first in my heart,
High God of heaven, my treasure thou art.

4. High God of heaven, my victory won;
May I reach heaven's joys, O bright heaven's Sun!
Heart of my own heart whatever befall,
Still be my vision, O Ruler of all.

Words used by permission as published in *Everflowing Streams*, ©1981,
The Pilgrim Press, New York, N.Y. "Slane," from the *Revised Church Hymnary*, 1927,
by permission of Oxford University Press.

Love Your Enemies

Musings

It is true that so far as wealth gives time for ideal ends and exercise to ideal energies, wealth is better than poverty and ought to be chosen. But wealth does this in only a portion of the actual cases. Elsewhere the desire to gain wealth and the fear to lose it are our chief breeders of cowardice and propagators of corruption. There are thousands of conjectures in which a wealth-bound man must be a slave, whilst the man for whom poverty has no terrors becomes a freeman. Think of the strength which personal indifference to poverty would give us if we were devoted to unpopular causes. We need no longer hold our tongues or fear to vote the revolutionary or reformatory ticket. Our stocks might fall, our hopes of promotion vanish, our salaries stop, our club doors close in our faces; yet, while we lived, we would imperturbably bear witness to the spirit, and our example would help set free our generation. The cause would need its funds, but we its servants would be potent as we personally were contented with our poverty.

I recommend this matter to your serious pondering for it is certain that the prevalent fear of poverty among the educated classes is the worst moral disease from which our civilization suffers.

– *William James*

A military contractor gave us a job polishing the sickles of mr. Death

But that's not work for a man or a woman. So we took Mr. Death's sickles, broke them in two and made bicycles instead.

Now, Mr. Death's job is in Jeopardy and ours is miles from there.

At the present time in North America, the "peace through strength" ideology holds a dominant place in people's imaginations. It does so largely because we have not seriously considered the alternatives. The North American political and cultural ethos discourages us from doing so. In spite of this, enough work has been done internationally and among peace groups to enable us to think in terms of a "common security" option.

Common security is based on the understanding that if we make ourselves secure by making others insecure, our "security" ultimately incites the aggression of those other people. We are only secure when others around us, around the world, feel secure. No one is secure until everyone is secure.

Security is here broadened beyond a militaristic definition. Security, like peace in the opening workshops, requires a just sharing of power and material possibilities for those people presently excluded. The internal unrest that leads to so much military intervention often begins as a justice issue; and it cries out to be solved as a justice issue. When not treated as such, the unrest eventually becomes a military issue. The Mohawks at Oka, the Palestinians in Israel, the peasants in Latin America remind us of this. Only when security is understood to include justice, does security become another word for "peace."

Mr Jobs gave me a job and picked my pocket, my heart pocket, and put it in a killer rocket — already fueled with a million hearts. But he feeds me well with sugar tarts

Here's great news for all of us. Free trade means we get a bigger piece of the American economy — and that includes — the whole military pie.

92 Love Your Enemies

WORKSHOP 8

"See my finger, see my thumb, see my missile – you'd better run!": the dogma of deterrence.

One of the most common arguments peacemakers face is that aggression is best discouraged by threatening equal or greater aggression. It is the belief that we deter by a readiness to *inter*.

The assumption is that the main cause of violent conflict or war preparations is simply the failure of the aggressor to clearly calculate the cost of aggression. When we respond with threats and intimidation, the aggressor (who we can assume is "them" and not "us") is expected to become more "reasonable" and clear-headed about the consequences of his actions.

Deterrence implies a great trust, if not faith, in the power of intimidation and the power to kill. Deterrence places its trust in death and the technologies of death. What may at very best "work" on rare occasions has become the ruling creed. The reduction of complex economic, religious, and political differences to a strictly military problem makes more profound analysis or response unlikely. Deterrence discounts what leads up to violent conflict. It is short-sighted about "solutions." Nevertheless, it persists as an argument that must be dealt with. This workshop is designed to help bring that about.

Objectives:
- To clarify our understanding of militarism's main dogma – the power of fear.
- To make us more confident to respond to arguments based on this dogma.

PART A

(4 min.)

Activity 1 – Warm Up
(These exercises should be done crisply without rushing.)

Repeat exercise with "dove" picture from workshop 3.

(8 min.)

Activity 2
"Mirror exercise." In pairs, people stand facing one another. They will take turns being a mirror to the other's actions . . . imitating their every move. Whoever moves first should begin with slow hand and arm gestures in order to give the partner opportunity to follow. Once your partner is comfortable, the first mover can move using more of the body and the face. The task of the "mirror" is to concentrate on the other. After a couple of minutes the animator can announce the changing of roles. (The objective of this exercise is to playfully nurture cooperation.)

(5 min.)

Activity 3
The "Pop, Fizz, How Sweet It Is" Wonder Machine. The group makes a circle. The animator asks someone to enter the circle and to begin making the movement and sound of their choice. The others are then invited to add their movement and sound, one at a time, until the wonder machine is complete.

PART B

(12 min.)

Activity 1
Each person is given two cartoons. Working alone, they are asked to take the cartoon of Samson and to assume the postures of the four figures – one at a time, of course. Keeping the positions for at least a half-minute each, they are first asked to imagine a sound and second, a thought that might flow from a person in that position. After having moved from the posture of one character to another, they are asked to write their sound and thought beside each character in the picture. This process is repeated for the other cartoon, as well. Folks should be reminded that there is no one correct answer to this exercise.

(15 min.)

Activity 2
In groups of three, invite people to share whatever they came up with. Then, have them pick one of the cartoons to share with the total group. Enjoy.

PART C

(5 min.)

Activity 1
The preceding exercise will have laid the groundwork for the group reading that is to follow. Everyone is given copies of the following excerpt from Phillips P. Moulton's *Ammunition for Peacemakers* (one of the five books that should be in every peacemaker's library.)

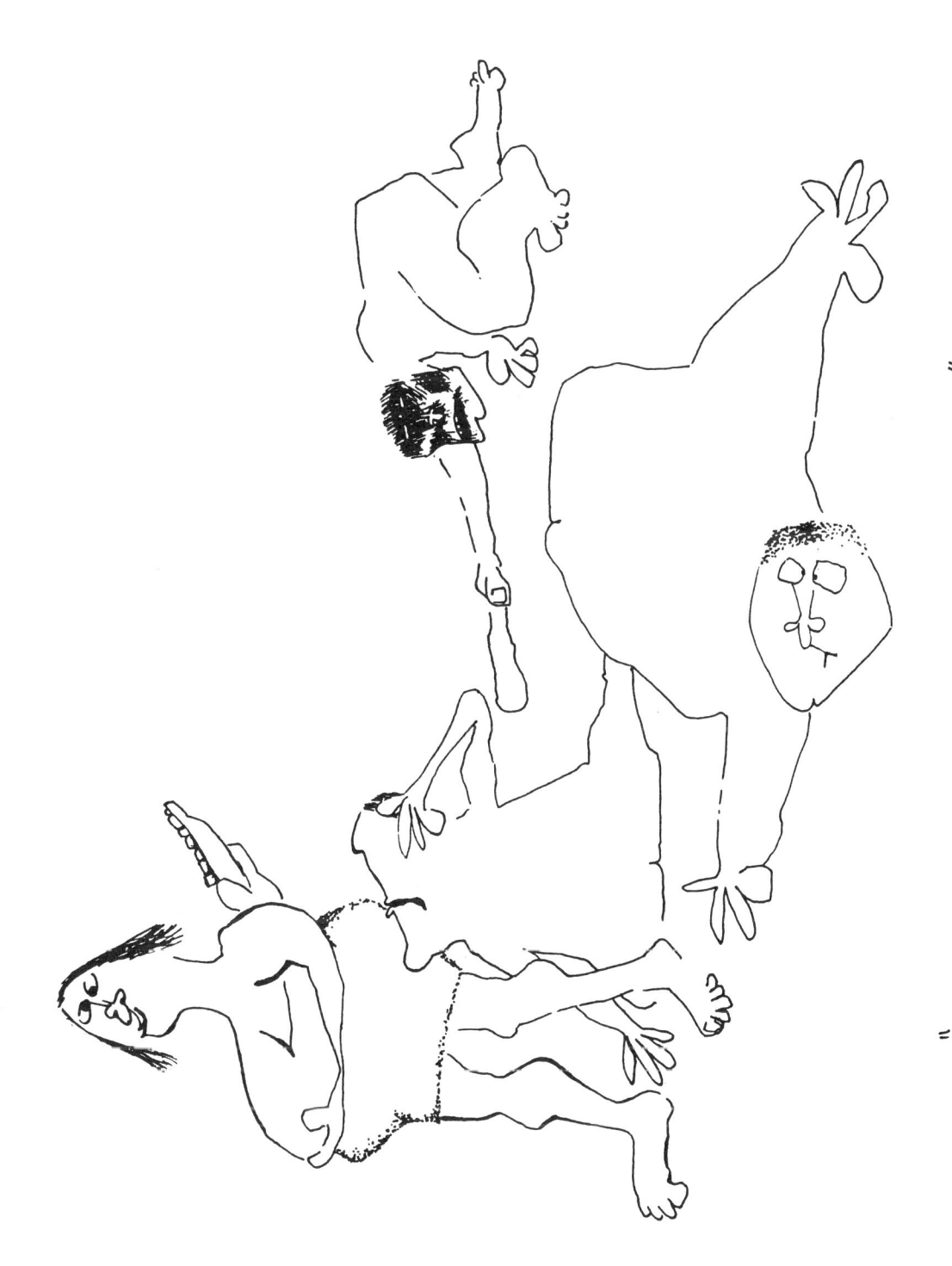

"With the jaw bone of an ass, Samson ass-ended them."

Workshop 8

Love Your Enemies

Limitations and Defects of Deterrence Strategy

The crucial question is not whether military might has any deterrent effect, but rather, What are its *total* effects? To get a comprehensive picture, the positive needs to be balanced against the negative. When this is done, it becomes evident that in today's world, military might is more provocative than deterrent.

1. *Survival not always considered the highest value.* A basic weakness in the deterrence theory is its lack of realism in assuming that the rival nation will place survival above all other values – that the fear of destruction will prevent if from attacking. Other motives or considerations may outweigh survival. For example, a jingoistic sense of national honour or a false concept of patriotism could easily take precedence. So could a deep sense of injustice or religious fanaticism. . . .

A nation may launch an attack and accept the risk of destruction out of sheer desperation if it thinks that its situation is intolerable or deteriorating seriously. It is then ranking higher than survival the values it is lacking or thinks it is losing. . . .

The deterrence doctrine rests on the assumption that the fear of destruction will prevent a leader from launching an attack. But any one of several motivating factors could out-weigh that fear. Arms strategists provide us with no answer to this criticism.

2. *Decision-makers not always thoroughly rational.* A second weakness in the deterrence theory is its assumption that the decision-makers of *all* nuclear powers will *always* be thoroughly rational. This is wishful thinking. It fails to recognize how irrational people are much of the time. . . . Within a few years, additional nations will be able to produce the bomb. Can it be assumed that all their leaders will invariably be guided by reflective and thoroughly realistic judgments?

The macho reaction would be a probable cause of war. Decision-makers may be driven by the desire to appear tough, to avoid being labelled appeasers, by unwillingness to back down when faced with an ultimatum. This powerful human tendency could cause a leader to risk catastrophe rather than lose face in the eyes of peers and constituents. During the Cuban missile crisis, this was apparently a factor in the refusal of President Kennedy's advisers to consider seriously Adlai Stevenson's proposal for a compromise solution.

When Admiral Hyman Rickover commissioned the first Trident submarine, with its 192 nuclear warheads and total explosive power of 2.4 million tons of TNT, he exulted that it would strike "fear and terror in the hearts of the enemy." Common sense tells us that terror and anxiety are not conducive to rational thought and action. This is confirmed by the studies of psychologists and sociologists. The more we threaten the Soviet leaders, the less secure they become; in response, they threaten us more, making us less secure. In today's world, the only true security is shared security.

Note this contradiction: Deterrence is based on the assumption that a potential opponent will be thoroughly rational; yet the military threat this is supposed to be the deterrent creates insecurity that breeds irrationality. Our policy-makers have not dealt adequately with this contradiction.

Such factors as emotional strain, fatigue, drug usage, or mental instability could also distort rational judgement enough to set missiles flying. In *Thirteen Days*, his memoir of the Cuban missile crisis, Robert F. Kennedy writes:

> *The strain and hours without sleep were beginning to take their toll . . . Each one of us was being asked to make a recommendation which would affect the future of all mankind . . . That kind of pressure does strange things to a human being, even to . . . mature, experienced men . . . The pressure is too overwhelming. . . . Some . . . even appeared to lose their judgment and stability.*

3. *Human error or miscalculation could trigger war.* In addition to the irrational decisions and error that could result from the factors just mentioned are the miscalculations that people make even under the best conditions.

In the name of deterrence, we pile up more nuclear weapons, disperse them more widely, and deploy them in more threatening situations. "Peace through strength" we proclaim. But this method of keeping the peace depends on no one making a crucial error in judgment or communication – or miscalculating the motives or reactions of potential enemies. Yet a common thread running through studies of wars and international crises is that miscalculations are often involved in their origins and escalation. Hugh Henning, director of the British Atlantic Committee, has rightly pointed out the miscalculation by the aggressor at the start of both world wars. The aggressors thought they could get away with actions that rivals were determined not to allow. . . .

4. *Technical malfunction could precipitate war.* A fourth unrealistic aspect of the deterrence doctrine is its fantastic optimism in assuming that no technical or mechanical failure will trigger a holocaust. Innumerable false alarms have occurred over the past twenty years. In re-

sponse, U.S. bombers have warmed up, tactical fighter aircraft have been launched, intercontinental ballistic missile units have gone on alert, and, in at least one instance, a command and control plane took off to direct operations. In each case, it took from three to six minutes of frenzied checking to determine that no Soviet missiles were en route. (Reliable information is lacking regarding the nature and frequency of similar occurrences on the Soviet side.)

5. *A combination of factors could touch off a war.* One might well ask why miscalculations or errors have not yet produced a nuclear war. One reason is that our officials have done a good job of creating redundant safety devices and measures that reduce the risk. On this basis, government spokespersons keep assuring us that unintended war is unlikely. They fail to note that war could erupt from a combination of factors during a military confrontation between the United States and the Soviet Union. If a series of false alarms had occurred during a major crisis, we would probably not be here today.

Reports published in October 1984 by experts in relevant fields who make up the Working Group on Unintentional Nuclear War of the International Physicians for the Prevention of Nuclear War (IPPNW) summarize the danger: "We live with the unacceptable high risk of inadvertent nuclear war, and ... this risk is increasing." After listing several reasons for this, such as the lack of effective U.S.-USSR communications and crisis management programs, they emphasize the impossibility of preventing every type of malfunction. They note that precautions and safety devices that are apparently adequate for every conceivable situation may not be adequate for a series of inconceivable coincidences.

They cite the power blackout in the northeastern United States and Ontario in 1965 and the accident at the Three Mile Island nuclear power plant in 1979. In each case, many precautions had been taken in the system design. After the power blackout, it was claimed that modifications made it impossible for such an accident to occur again. But in July 1977, a succession of lightning strikes that "just never happen" (to quote the president of Consolidated Edison Company) knocked out the New York part of the system. The IPPNW Working Party concludes: "The most significant risk ... seems to come from the possibility of a combination of an international crisis, mutually-reinforcing alerts, and possible computer failure and human error."

It should be emphasized that the arms buildup largely responsible for the danger of unintended war is invariably rationalized by reference to the doctrine of deterrence. For example, many of the U.S. nuclear weapons are designed at the Lawrence Livermore National Laboratory in California. The former public affairs director of the laboratory states that the scientists are "sharp people . . . very competitive with the laboratory at Los Alamos." It is in their interest "to be very creative about the kinds of weapons they come up with so that they get more contracts." They prefer not to be pictured as being in the weapons business, but when asked about it, they give the standard reply: "We're involved in deterrence. . . . The only way to achieve peace is . . . from a position of strength." (When the public affairs director came to realize that he and his colleagues were deceiving themselves, he resigned.) . . .

6. *Military power more provocative than deterrent.* We have noted that the dominant U.S. policymakers and defense analysts think within a narrow range of traditional assumptions that do not take adequate account of the radically different situation that nuclear weapons have thrust upon us. This is especially evident when one considers the whole range of effects of the arms buildup. On the surface, it seems obvious that increasing U.S. military strength would deter potential aggressors. In a limited sense, perhaps it does. But it also has a provocative effect, which our leaders ignore. The primary question, then, is whether the provocation outweighs the deterrence.

Surprisingly, the advocates of military escalation as a deterrent scarcely consider how the Soviet Union will react. Piling up additional nuclear weapons does not increase U.S. security, for we are not alone in doing so. Our action provokes the Soviets to match or surpass us. It accelerates a dangerous arms race. Far from constituting a deterrent, the result is that each side is less secure than it was before.

In October 1981, President Reagan outlined a massive military expansion program. One of our most perceptive and loyal public servants, Paul C. Warnke, former director of the Arms Control and Disarmament Agency, testified before the Senate Foreign Relations Committee concerning that program. He made this astute observation:

> *In deciding on a new weapons system, we ought always to ask ourselves how we'll feel when the other side does the same, as they are sure to do. In deploying multiple independently targeted reentry vehicles in 1969, we exploited a temporary technological edge. But if MIRVed missiles had never been deployed, we would not today have any concerns about possible ICBM vulnerability. Before going ahead with sea-launched cruise missiles, we ought to consider a future time when we might have to regard every Soviet trawler or fishing boat as a strategic nuclear delivery vehicle. And I doubt that we could ever know, or devise a verification formula to count, the numbers of Soviet warheads on a sea-launched cruise missile force.*

A proposal to ban MIRVs (Multiple Independently Targeted Reentry Vehicles) and cruise missiles instead of developing them would almost certainly have been accepted by the Soviets: Their technology was behind ours; their overburdened economy needed relief; they have a realistic fear of the holocaust such weapons bring closer.

U.S. deployment of ever more speedy and accurate nuclear weapons incites the Soviets to threaten us in like fashion. As the readiness to strike intensifies on both sides and a crisis develops, suppose the strategists of one side conclude that war is imminent. They then face two alternatives: if they hesitate, they will risk the unimpaired might of the enemy. If they strike first, they will greatly reduce the opponent's destructive power. They will have a tremendous incentive to launch a preemptive attack. "Use them or lose them" will be the cry. The other side will react in similar fashion, producing the scenario posed by Thomas C. Schelling, professor at the Kennedy School of Government, Harvard University: "He, thinking I was about to kill him in self-defense, was about to kill me in self-defense, so I had to kill him in self-defense...."

7. *Vertical proliferation stimulates horizontal proliferation.* In still another way, seeking deterrence by enlarging our nuclear stockpiles increases the danger of war more than it prevents it. It encourages additional nations to get nuclear weapons. The reasons for this are evident.

After all, if nuclear weapons allegedly provide peace through strength for the United States, why should this not be true for others? President Saddam Hussein of Iraq has openly declared that the Arabs need the bomb for this very purpose. And just as the United States is now accumulating nuclear weapons not only to deter, but also to initiate or fight a war, if deterrence fails, Third World nations naturally conclude that such weapons would also be useful in actual combat.

Moreover, the very possession of nuclear arms by the major powers gives the weapons a prestige value in the eyes of smaller nations. The first nuclear explosion by France was welcomed by Charles de Gaulle with the boast that France became "stronger and prouder" that day. As Bernard Goldschmidt, who publicized the technology of reprocessing plutonium, declared, "If you wanted to be somebody in this world, you had to have a bomb."

It is ironic that trying to prevent war by supposedly improving our nuclear deterrent actually has the opposite effect. In respect to proliferation, the technology that brings smaller, cheaper weapons makes it easier for other nations to manufacture them. Our development of cruise missiles, for example, provides the know-how for nations that could not afford the larger, more expensive rockets....

8. *Summary of limitations.* The preceding discussion reveals the irony of the concept of deterrence, on which U.S. foreign policy is allegedly based. It is probably true that the massive stockpiling of nuclear weapons tends to deter a rational ruler from starting a war when there is ample time for reflection and no crisis exists. But that is the least likely way a nuclear war might start. Strengthening nuclear capabilities to guard against that one unlikely scenario greatly increases the probability of war starting in other ways.

Despite allegedly deterrent arsenals, national leaders may start a war because of one (or a combination) of these factors:

- They believe that values more important than survival are at stake – national honor, patriotism, freedom, justice, or religion.
- They do not always act rationally. Their decisions may be affected by macho reactions, fear, anxiety, and other emotional factors.
- Human errors and miscalculations become more likely as nuclear weapons become more numerous and complex.
- Technical or mechanical failures could produce misleading signals, or a computer error in a launch-on-warning system could set missiles flying.
- The buildup on one side provokes similar action by the adversary, increasing the likelihood of a dangerous confrontation.
- The proliferation of nuclear weapons gives to additional nations the means to wage a disastrous war, which could involve the superpowers.

What defense strategists overlook is that the possible deterrent effect of nuclear striking power is far outweighed by the increasing peril it creates. If we removed the deterrent, the Soviets would almost certainly remove theirs (see chapter III). Our world would then be much safer.

Activity 2

(25 min.)

The role-play exercise, based on the group reading, could be introduced like this:

Congratulations! You have been hired as the researcher for a nationwide radio talkshow. Your job is to prepare the host, Erika Ritter, for an upcoming interview. She will be interviewing a respected spokesperson who opposes the "Peace through strength" ideology and its dogma of deterrence.

The spokesperson will be speaking at a public forum tomorrow night. You have a copy of selections from that speech (the Moulton material, above). Your task is to read through these selections making a one-line summary of each paragraph. If you have time, suggest your own title for these selections

– *something catchy. This will be used to brief Erika on the position. Erika, or her personal assistant, arrives in twenty-five minutes to hear your summary. Get as much done as you can manage.*

(10 min.)

Activity 3
If you are not Erika Ritter, you may be able to pass yourself off as her personal assistant. In any case, the task remains: as a total group, walk through the article, asking for a sentence summary for each paragraph, writing down the sentence or key words. The objective is to make sure folks are grasping the important information and lines of argument. The facilitator should repeat aloud the key ideas since repetition aids memory. Ask that questions, at this point, relate only to written ideas, i.e., questions of clarification. The ideas themselves will be discussed shortly.

(6 min.)

Activity 4
Quickly elicit from the group some standard slogans of Deterrence Dogma. For example, "Walk softly and carry a big stick;" or "The only thing they understand is force." (I assume that we are so immersed in this dogma that the catch-phrases will act as a catalyst for the upcoming role-play.)

PART D

(12 min.)

Activity 1 – First Role Play
Working in pairs, folks are asked to take turns being the spokesperson and the radio interviewer. The spokesperson's task is to present objections to Deterrence policy. The interviewer is a sympathetic listener yet aware of the Deterrence claims. The interviewer's task is to ask questions that will clarify the spokesperson's views, not critique them. Each person should "have a go" at each role. (The objective is to help everyone make these basic observations their own; also to help folks become more comfortable conversing on the deterrence debate.) Each should share how he or she experienced the role-playing before we move on.

(25 min.)

Activity 2 – Second Role Play
The total group makes a circle with a table and four chairs in the centre. The setting is a kitchen. Two volunteers are asked to begin a conversation. One person is a defender of the Deterrence policy while the other is an opponent. The role players' objective is not to "win" an argument but to be able to understand as clearly as possible the other position.

There are two empty chairs so that some may enter the conversation and others may leave it when they wish. If someone wants to enter the

Workshop 8

conversation when the chairs are full, they simply tag a player and take their position. After the role-play has had time to develop, assign someone to introduce the second topic – "How does Christ's teaching about the love of enemies give us direction, insofar as we claim to be a Christian nation?"

Participants should be given an opportunity to de-role, followed by a round of applause to end this section.

PART E

(18 min.)

Worship

1. Words of Gathering:

Let us be gathered in the good company of the Creator and Redeemer of the earth, in whose presence we are given rest, and a divine restlessness for the healing of the nations, and all the earth. Amen.

2. The following exercise should take place in a circle with everyone standing. It seeks to create physical expressions or metaphors for the refusal of peace and for the seeking of peace. Everyone is asked to close their eyes and let their arms hang by their sides.

Let each hand slowly tighten into a fist. Feel the anger at those whom you fall into argument with. Feel the wish to hit those who hit you with words, looks, threats of different kinds. Feel the deep fears that your fists embody. Sense the tightness of your fists, your arms, your neck. Sense the energy it takes to maintain that readiness for violence. Sense how the fist-weapons organize and align the rest of your body to their purpose.

This inflexible posture we are in, is the posture of a nation whose foreign policy is based on intimidation and threat.

Turn to the person next to you. Press your fists against theirs. Feel the points and hardness of their fists with your fists. Remaining there, place your fists in front of your face, about a foot away from your face. Let your left hand slowly unfold like a flower before the morning sun. Now let your right fist slowly unfold. Now shake your hands and forearms, and then, shake your whole arms by your sides.

Let each person take one of their neighbour's hands. Rub the palm and fingers, getting a sense of the relative softness and roundness of that hand which was hidden in a fist. This is the posture of nations that have the courage to be open to each other.

Let us applaud one another and then sit down for a short reading.

3. *Our reading is from the gospel as told to us by Luke. It speaks to us of an incident after Christ's resurrection. Two of Christ's followers encounter Christ but do not recognize him, as they walk along a road near the village of Emmaus. Christ, a stranger even to his followers, walks along with them, talking. They see only a stranger, a potential enemy. Yet they are not possessed by the kind of fear that makes strangers into enemies.*

It is the spirit-filled, open-handed hospitality of Christ's followers to this stranger that allows love and mercy to appear; love and mercy incarnate and resurrected. Listen for the moment God's presence flowers forth. (Read Luke 24:13-17, 28-31a.)

4. *O night-bringing, day-breaking Creator, you are mystery to our cleverness, to our deathly cold calculations. To fists pounding like hammers, or hanging hopelessly by sides, you are the open hands giving the bread of life. You are the open hands nailed to the cross of history which are then unfurled like roses before Thomas' touch.*

As people who make our own fists, or who accommodate the making of national nuclear fists, we come to you with our prayers of confession, spoken aloud or in the silence of our hearts. God, you who forgive the broken-hearted, we come to you with thanksgiving for organizations like the United Nations, insofar as they have helped nations discover more lasting and caring ways of settling differences. We give you thanks for churches and peace organizations that have not fuelled self-righteous condemnation of our enemies, but have sought ongoing dialogue which now bears small flowers of hope and for our own experience of hands opening to sisters, and brothers in this small gathering, we give you thanks.

Hear now as we pray for your world, your seekers after peace, and for ourselves in this . . .

In Christ's name, we ask it. Amen.

5. Song: "Be Not Afraid."

6. Benediction:

Let us each take our neighbour's hands and say: "May the blessings of Christ the peace-maker be yours this night, and for evermore."

Be Not Afraid

Words & Music by
Bob Dufford, S.J.

1. You shall cross the barren desert, but you shall not die of thirst. You shall wander far in safety though you do not know the way. You shall speak your words in foreign lands and all will understand. You shall see the face of God and live. (Antiphon)

ANTIPHON

Be not afraid. I go before you always. Come follow Me, and I will give you rest.

Copyright © 1975, 1978, Robert J. Dufford, S.J. and New Dawn Music, P.O. Box 13248, Portland, OR 97213-0248. All rights reserved. Used by permission.

Love Your Enemies

Be Not Afraid/cont.

2. If you pass through rag-ing wat-ers in the sea, you shall not drown. If you walk a-mid the burn-ing flames, you shall not be harmed. If you stand be-fore the pow'r of hell and death is at your side, know that I am with you through it all. (Antiphon)

3. Bless-ed are your poor for the king-dom shall be theirs. Blest are you that weep and mourn, for one day you shall laugh. And if wick-ed men in-sult and hate you all be-cause of Me, bless-ed, bless-ed are you! (Anitphon)

Workshop 8

Musings

Sometimes Jesus calls forth "laughter at," derisive laughter. Like the prophets, he corrects with harsher comedy, or satire. His satire contains anger at the powerful for their denial of God's graciousness. Jesus never uses satire against the poor. He uses it often against the self-serving religion of the middle and upper classes, represented by the scribes and Pharisees.

Come let us be gathered in worship of the God who laughs the mighty from the heights and leaves banana skins before our pride, the God for whom whales and giants are toys and the noise of our praise can be song.

Peaceable Commonwealth

Love Your Enemies

Inspired by fear of the Philistines, Israel buys a bigger and better sword

Musings

WORKSHOP 9

The farce of force: discovering our security in "Common Security."

An authority rules most easily when it rules the imagination of its people. Our imaginations can be ruled by being corrupted, or narrowed, so that we are only able to imagine that which the dominant order wants us to imagine. When "reality" is the best thing that we can "realistically" imagine, the ruling order is *most* effective. Under such circumstances there is no need for propaganda campaigns or police intimidation because our imaginations eventually police themselves.

At the present time in North America, the "peace through strength" ideology holds a dominant place in people's imaginations. It does so largely because we have not seriously considered the alternatives. The North American political and cultural ethos discourages us from doing so. In spite of this, enough work has been done internationally and among peace groups to enable us to think in terms of a "common security" option.

Common security is based on the understanding that if we make ourselves secure by making others insecure, our "security" ultimately incites the aggression of those other people. We are only secure when others around us, around the world, feel secure. No one is secure until everyone is secure.

Security is here broadened beyond a militaristic definition. Security, like peace in the opening workshops, requires a just sharing of power and material possibilities for those people presently excluded. The internal unrest that leads to so much military intervention often begins as a justice issue; and it cries out to be solved as a justice issue. When not treated as such, the unrest eventually becomes a military issue. The Mohawks at Oka, the Palestinians in Israel, the peasants in Latin America remind us of this. Only when security is understood to include justice, does security become another word for "peace." The task of our workshop is to explore the question of security more fully.

Objectives:

- To explore ways in which Christ's pattern of turning enemies into friends might translate into international relations.
- To provide an understanding of the alternatives to the dogma of nuclear deterrence.

PART A

(10 min.)

Activity 1 – Warm up

Play some quiet and slow to moderately paced music. Ask folks to walk in as large a circle as the space will allow. Intersperse their walking with a series of quietly spoken instructions:

As you walk, be aware of the heaviness, the weight of each foot . . . and its lightness. As you walk, slow down slightly and lengthen your step. Notice the weight, the heaviness of your step . . . notice its lightness. As you walk, exaggerate the movement of your shoulders and arms. Feel your arms swing. As you walk, move your shoulders up toward your ears and then down toward your ankles. Now, wiggle your hands and fingers.

As you walk, slow down to a standstill and take the sitting position that is most comfortable for you, on a chair or floor. Find a comfortable posture with your back straight, your palms open and upward, resting on your legs . . . close your eyes. Listen to the breathing of those around you. . . . Become aware of your own breathing in, breathing out . . . breathe deeply and slow it down. Remember, each of us is the body and breath God gives awhile. Listen now to a petition, a please, a plea. (Say it very slowly.) "May God's breath move in and out of each one here – as we gather to seek God's ways of peacemaking for all creatures of God's breath-filled creation." Amen.

PART B

(20 min.)

Activity 1 – Body-Sculpting Exercise

Body-sculpting offers a playful and non-cerebral change of pace. It will reveal much that words cannot – unless you are a poet. In order to get started it is useful to offer you own body as "clay." Best of all, this gives folks the opportunity to laugh at the "leader," which is always important. Then you too are taking some of the apparent "risk."

It should be pointed out that in introducing sculpting, the "clay," being clay, must be shaped the way the sculptor wants it: facial expression with mouth and eyes, back, arms, legs, and so on. It is in the shaping that the germ of an image or pose will develop and grow. So shape the clay and stand back. Look at it. Try two or three different poses. Some striking surprises often emerge.

Workshop 9

(25 min.)

Activity 2
To relax for this exercise we will warm up by trying to sculpt a figure based on three scenes I'm going to describe. I will be the clay; you be the sculptors.

- *You are house-sitting for a friend. It is a big old house and night has fallen. Outside, it is cold and rainy. You are sitting at the kitchen table, alone. You think you hear noises. You do. Noises coming from the basement. Uneven squeaky noises. But noises. You go to the basement door. You slowly open it. It is dark. You turn on the light to find that the basement floor is crawling with . . . rats.*

I am the clay. You are the sculptors. Will someone come up and sculpt me at that moment of first seeing the crawling squeaking vermin? I am only clay. (As the "clay," you remain standing in the centre, completely relaxed, arms hanging loosely at your side, head hanging down, eyes closed. Before inviting a second sculptor to come forward, hold the pose crafted by the first sculptor so everyone has a chance to walk around and view that sculptor's work. Hold the pose. Don't ham. Before you invite a second sculptor to try this scene, remind everyone to think in terms of using the back, shoulders, and feet, as well as face and hands.)

- *You have been driving for eight hours in heavy traffic with rain falling. As the rain begins to let up, you turn off the main road. You stop the car and get out at a small lake glistening with sun. You stand at the shore smelling the freshness of pine and listening to the song of two loons. You are drinking all this in. You are swimming in the light, smells, and sound.*

I am the clay. Sculpt me at that moment. (Repeat with a second sculptor, after which you might ask someone else to be clay for the final warm up.)

- *You are in a state of funk and have been all week. Body cold, feeling down, home alone watching the endless cloud and cold rain drooling down the window panes. Your closest friend, with whom you share so much, is away in Europe for another two weeks. And the forecast is for more rain (and personal funk). There's a knock at the door. You open it to find your best friend, home early and beaming as he or she passes you a handful of flowers. Sculpt yourself at that moment. "Mary" is the clay. You are the sculptor.*

(15 min.)

Activity 3
Your reputation as sculptor has spread abroad. Tomorrow morning you will receive a registered letter from the ecumenical peace organization, Project Ploughshares. The letter asks you to create a three-figure sculpture to be placed on the front lawn of the Parliament Buildings in Ottawa. It is to be entitled, "Things that make for war."

In preparation: make yourself comfortable and then close your eyes a moment. Imagine a three-figure sculpture entitled, "Things that make for war." "Mary," "John," and "Susan" have agreed to be clay for the first while. Can we have a sculptor? (Ask folks to hold their pose until everyone has had an opportunity to walk around and view the sculpture... and for you to snap a polaroid or two. Repeat exercise once or twice more, inviting applause at the deconstruction of each sculpture.)

Activity 4

(30 min.)

Your sculpture has received world-wide recognition. There is even talk of your artwork being used on a sweat shirt and on lawn ornaments. (This makes you a little nervous about whether people have grasped the spirit of your creative labours.) Then, one day you receive a registered letter from the United Nations. You are being asked to create a three- or four-piece sculpture with the working title: "What makes for peace between nations?"

There is one complication. You are asked not to begin until you study a short document on relations between nations. The document consists of a series of excerpts from a work on peacemaking produced by PROJECT PEACE-MAKERS, an ecumenically-funded research and education project in Canada.

Underlying the insight of this document is the awareness from scripture – evidenced by Amos, Isaiah, the Gospels, etc. – of the need to undermine the arrogance of nations; especially those who think their constant use of God's name justifies the preparation for and practice of violence. The national illusion of superiority discourages these nations from seeing their enemies as God's children. Their illusion needs to be undermined.

In order to help nations, especially those that use God's name, to see the wideness of God's mercy and creation, the document opposes the view that enemy nations are cesspools of evil. An approach that turns enemies into friends becomes a central concern. The document preparing you for your sculpture, "The things that make for peace," follows this particular biblical pattern.

A proposed method for reading that will prepare you for sculpting goes as follows:

- *Read through the piece once, quickly.*

- *On second reading, make a one-line summary of each paragraph in the margin.*

- *Share two key ideas with one other person. Help one another unfold the implications of those ideas.*

Common Security

The phrase "common security" has come into wide usage in recent years. Because it is not a technical term, it has acquired a variety of meanings, all of which represent variations on the theme: "we're all in it together." In other words, our security ultimately depends on co-operation in human development rather than competition. This acknowledges that state or national "security" is not a supreme human value. Our primary obligation is to honour and protect human life and well-being. There are strict limits to the means that are acceptable in defence of states and other transitory human institutions....

One implication of the Common Security approach is that security is mutual rather than competitive. That is, one's own security is enhanced by the security of others and our own security cannot be purchased with the insecurity of others.

This is the opposite of what might be called "fortress security," in which one attempts, within a hostile environment, to build a wall within which one can be protected from external threats. Common security finds fortress security ultimately futile and destructive. The economic cost of its militarization destroys human social and economic security and in the process brutalizes societies through an inevitable erosion of human and political rights.

The nuclear "fortress" is a clear example of this futile process. The drive to build the most threatening nuclear weapons makes us all hostage to the threat of mass destruction and even annihilation. Thus, at a minimum, mutual security asserts that nuclear and other weapons of mass destruction have no place in national or international defence policies.

National security cannot be assured in isolation. It is ultimately not possible to isolate and cushion one's self from a hostile environment. Attempts to do so, whether with a military buffer like the one that the Soviet Union has in Europe, or with a technological "shield" like the U.S. Star Wars project, only stimulate more fear and more threats in response. Instead, national security is assured in common with others through measures to transform the social and political environment itself. Peace is the fruit of a just international order. Canadian security is no exception. Canadian security relies ultimately, not on Canada's ability to defend itself militarily, but on an international order that recognizes and respects Canadian sovereignty and territorial integrity....

Collective security declares that the security of individual states is the business of all states and that this, far from being evidence of the weakness of individual states, is evidence of our common humanity and mutual concern.

It was collective security in this sense that was central to the original vision of the United Nations. Through this world body, states would collectively guarantee the security of individual states, not primarily by direct military means, but by non-military means of collectively disciplining those states that threatened the integrity of others.

World security needs to be based on the same assumptions with which we order our neighbourhoods. In our communities, the security of individual homes is deemed to be a collective, not individual, responsibility. When an intruder enters our home, we are not obliged to single-handedly deal with the intruder – rather we are obliged to call the community security forces to come to our aid. This is not, however, to say that individual citizens, or individual states, do not have responsibilities to contribute to collective security measures. The primary contribution is to maintain one's own home in such a manner as to reduce the likelihood of intruders. Doors and windows need to be locked so as not to invite intrusion. . . .

Heavily militarized states, or states based on blatantly unjust social arrangements and in which human rights are abused, invite a cycle of abuse, dissent, repression of dissent, greater abuse and so on, until domestic "security" is destroyed and the security of the region is threatened. In other words, what happens in one state has implications for others. And thus the collective security of states requires that individual states have a minimal responsibility to ensure that they are not a fire-trap within the international community and thus a threat to the security of neighbours. This means, in the case of Canada, a recognition that Canadian territory, given its strategic place between the two superpowers, can be a means of either stabilizing or threatening the international order.

One of the ways in which a nation state can become a "neighbourhood firetrap" is to permit it to be used by third parties for the purpose of attacking or threatening others – thus, Canadian territory should not be made available to any other country for the purpose of attacking or threatening to attack a third country.

True collective security requires the development of a collective security institution that is capable of protecting individual countries and of disciplining states that threaten to attack others. National security should not be the sole responsibility of each nation state.

The present international system is the equivalent of each household stocking an arsenal of weapons, conducting family shooting practice and joining a neighbourhood vigilante group (our term for this is a military alliance). This is a formula for uninterrupted and extreme militarization.

Each state feels the need to demonstrate sufficient firepower to deal with real or potential threats. The neighbours, seeing that firepower, feel threatened and so too arm themselves (and sometimes the better armed are tempted to go out on to the street to swagger and exercise a bit of power in the neighbourhood). The spiral continues and internally the entire social order is brutalized.

Activity 4 (4 min.)
Having spent ten minutes sharing ideas, sit quietly by yourself with eyes closed and think on your sculpture entitled "Things that make for peace." After a time, imagine three or four large mounds of clay. Imagine the rough shapes you might give them. In your own little space with your own little body physically assume something of each of those shapes.

Activity 5 (20 min.)
Have the whole group arrange themselves in a circle. Ask for volunteers to be "clay." Invite would-be sculptors to take turns. Have the clay people hold their poses so that the others can walk around and view the sculpture. Ask for applause after every creation (whether to celebrate it or to chase it away).

Activity 6 (15 min.)
After five or six attempts, ask people which sculptures or parts of the sculptures most helped them to understand or imagine "what makes for peace." Discuss.

Activity 7 (15 min.)
If time permits, ask the group if there were any images or thoughts from the common security article which they wanted to sculpt that didn't develop or get fully formed. Have them share these partially-formed images one at a time. Invite the group to brainstorm ways of sculpting the ideas being presented.

PART C

(30 min.)

Worship

The worship will be conducted around a bowl of grape juice or wine. In front of each person is a tablespoon and a small or medium-sized glass resting on a small dish.

1. Words of Gathering:

Come, let us be gathered in the good company of saints and other sinners . . . the company that reaches back to the beginning of time. Be gathered with Abraham, Sarah, and Hagar and the great parade of those who have struggled to be faithful; faithful to the Creator of the earth and all the nations. Be gathered with those in our time, from every nation, who work for the healing of the nations. Be gathered in the good company of God's daughters and sons who are behind us and beside us, ahead of us . . .

surrounding us. Be gathered in God's good company, to praise and ponder the mercy of God.

2. Let us pray:

O Holy Creator, passionate for the well-being of your whole creation; troubled at the people's rejection of your grace and freedom; sorrowful at the nations' love of death and attraction to oblivion, blessed be your presence.

Hear our confession, of turning, turning away from your alarming passion for the well-being of your earth and its peoples.

Hear the confession of our hearts . . . (time for reflection) . . . O mystery, O mercy, forgive us and heal our sickness of Spirit. Help us find our security in your gifts of breath and daily bread, no longer drawn to our heroes' promise of economic security or military security. Help us find our security in you and the signs of your Spirit's presence that surround us in the everyday . . . everyday signs of compassion and resistance to injustice; the dignity you seek for all your children maintained amidst misery; green blades of grass squeezing through cracks in the cement. Grant us hearts to see and wonder at your grace that touches us minute by minute. In Christ's name, we ask it. Amen.

3. *In a few moments everyone is going to be invited to share the names of companions, ancient or modern, groups or individuals, who give us a sense of direction or courage. As we share these companions with the group let us share a little description of what it is that makes them important to us. After each person has spoken, let us dip our spoons into the common bowl, and then place a spoonful of wine/juice into our glasses. This is accompanied by the refrain written on the sheet taped to the wall: "Even though we walk in the valley of the shadow of death . . . Our cups runneth over."*

After each member of the group has shared one or two of their saints, you can put a second question to them:

As we continue filling our cups/glasses, can each of us share an everyday occasion that speaks of God's presence?

Once each person has had an opportunity to share (or the liberty not to share), ask them to take turns putting their neighbour's glass to their neighbour's lips so that each may be given a first sip. As folks continue sipping from their own glasses, give them time to talk with one another about companions or occasions shared.

4. Song: "Drops of Water."

5. Benediction:

Go, now, in the good company of the saints and other sinners, undiscovered friends, hidden companions, some guy named Elijah, and God the Father who mothers us, the Holy Spirit and Christ, our brother and hope. Amen.

Drops Of Water

From the teachings of Jesus and Ghandi

Words and Music by Jim Strathdee

We are drops of wa-ter in a might-y o-cean,
We are sons and daugh-ters of one life. life.

1. Be ye not a-fraid of what to-mor-row brings; Keep your mind on God's

© Copyright 1977 by Desert Flower Music, P.O. Box 1476, Carmichael, CA 95605.
Used by permission.

Drops of Water/cont.

2. Empty all yourself. Listen and be still,
   Let God's holy spirit lead you where it will,
   Like the rushing waters fill your soul,
   Let the truth within you grow, in you grow.
   (Chorus)

3. You are not alone, your suffering we bear,
   Ev'rybody's vict'ry is a victory we share,
   The tiny drop of water dies all alone,
   But the ocean of love will overcome, overcome.
   (Chorus)

PART D

(5 min.)

Reading and Homework Assignment

Living in a consumer society, we will be inclined to treat what we've discovered during the last nine weeks as just another interesting bit of information. But now we know that to see an injustice and not respond to it is to harden our heart, thereby becoming less of a person. On the other hand, when we respond to injustice, often without the assurance of success, we become God's compassionate creatures, as we are called to be.

Our action may make a difference in the world today, or the day after tomorrow, or, it may not make a difference. Nevertheless, inaction, or turning away from what we know, makes a major difference to who we are as people. Inaction splits us further in two, separating our heart and hands, mind and feet. If Christ calls to us to be peacemakers and we accept, we experience integration and integrity. Action itself will not make us good, but it will unite our beliefs with who we are.

What each of us is called upon to become and to do is something we need to work out between ourselves and our relation to Christ and God's spirit. Similarly, we need to work this out in relation to our neighbours, from whom Christ never separates his Spirit.

What follows is a list of some typical actions for peacemakers from a chapter in Working for Peace, *edited by Neil Wollman. Some are big, some small.*

1. Our first task is to go through the list, writing beside each item – N (for "never"), M (for "maybe"), Y (for "yes, I can do that"). After you've worked through the list, try to add items of your own, as you think about your own abilities and circumstances.

2. Can you identify two actions you would like to take?

3. As you consider the kind of peacemaker you would like to become, what do you need to do differently?

4. What do you need to stop doing?

5. What do you need to continue?

Building Confidence for Social Action

Like any other kind of learning, learning to be active and effective in response to peace issues takes time. You can learn by reading and by talking with others who are more experienced, but most of all, you learn by doing. Social action at its best represents an attempt by you (alone or with others) to bring your particular interests and talents to bear on a problem of your own choosing. Generally, social action can be classified as research, education, or direct action.

Following is a list of social actions in which people engage. You will need to duplicate the list in some form. There are several purposes for the list. It is intended to help you (a) assess your unique interests and skills in relation to social action, (b) evaluate the difficulties that particular kinds of activities present, so that you can better understand them, and (c) help you choose the most appropriate tasks and build confidence in undertaking them.

The list can be used most effectively in a support group, with sharing of experiences and mutual exploration of problems and options, but it can also be used alone. In the former case, there should be no pressure to achieve or to conform. The best results will be obtained if you can make an honest assessment of what you wish to do, unpressured by others' expectations.

1. Join a national organization that is active on peace issues.
2. Write a letter to the editor of a local paper encouraging people to think about a peace issue.
3. Spend several hours a week doing volunteer office work for a peace organization.
4. Obtain a peace-related slide show to present to my church group.
5. Encourage my local political party to endorse peace policies.
6. Ask some friends to come to my home and discuss a peace issue.
7. Write a letter to my member of parliament urging him/her to vote a certain way on an upcoming bill.
8. Spend time learning about organizations that work on a particular issue so that I can discuss the groups with others.
9. Circulate among my friends a petition supporting action on a peace-related problem.
10. Raise funds for a cause by organizing an event (a garage sale, a bake sale, a walk or run, a book sale, a craft fair, etc.).
11. Write a letter to a government official, criticizing her/his decision on an issue.
12. Set aside 20 minutes a day to think about and study an issue, and consider what I can do about it.
13. Talk about a peace issue with someone I just met at a party.
14. Write a letter to the editor of a local paper criticizing actions of the city council or a local business firm that contribute to a spirit of violence.

15. Join a social action group that is not too popular in my community because of its outspokenness on a peace issue.

16. Make it a point to bring a peace issue into conversations whenever the opportunity presents itself.

17. Think about my own particular interests and skills, and figure out how I can contribute to solving a global conflict problem and enjoy myself at the same time.

18. Organize a speakers bureau in my community.

19. Persuade several friends to join a group to which I belong.

20. Take an unpopular position on an issue that arose during a local civic group meeting I attended.

21. Send a gift subscription of a peace-oriented magazine to a friend that might be interested.

22. Explore how people in my profession can contribute to peace.

23. Withhold a percentage of my taxes to protest government spending that contributes to a military conflict.

24. Talk with my minister about directing certain church funds toward peacemaking.

25. Write a letter to a magazine journalist criticizing her/his article.

26. Stop buying a product that I know is produced by exploiting poor people in another country.

27. Write a letter to my member of parliament criticizing militaristic statements he or she made at a news conference.

28. Join a non-violent demonstration obstructing the gates of a nearby defense plant.

29. Call in to radio talk shows to express a peace concern.

30. Set up a booth at a community or county fair to provide literature and talk with people about militarism.

31. Help a group to which I belong plan a public meeting on a peace issue.

32. Volunteer for a low-paying job with a peace group overseas.

33. Run a newspaper ad regularly about world conflict.

34. Prepare an annotated reading list on an issue to distribute among friends and groups to which I belong.

35. Join a peace demonstration marching through the middle of town, knowing the stance is not popular with local people.
36. Telephone my MP or MLA to convey my peace concerns.
37. Canvass local business, asking permission to place a peace sign (or a sign publicizing a local group) in their window.
38. Actively help plan a demonstration at a local defense-related industry.
39. Feed and house people who come to my area to speak or do other peace work.
40. Write a letter to the president of a large corporation to complain about its ties to military defense.
41. Canvass the neighborhood door-to-door to raise funds or survey attitudes about peace.
42. Try to arrange a dialogue between opposing factions in a dispute about peace.
43. Appear on a TV talk show to discuss a peace issue.
44. Be a part of a phone tree to alert people to a peace issue needing urgent action.
45. Organize a rally in a local park to protest government action in a conflict somewhere in the world.
46. Write to national radio and TV networks urging them to carry a program on war and peace.
47. Contribute part of my monthly budget to a peace-related cause.
48. Explore ways to introduce war and peace issues into the curriculum of local schools.
49. Purchase and distribute materials on conflict wherever I think they might create some interest.
50. Write a grant proposal for money to develop a local peace program.
51. Take part in a march across the country to make people more aware of an issue.
52. Become known as a person willing to speak about peace.
53. Organize a benefit concert with area musicians to raise funds for a cause.
54. Volunteer my vacation time to work on a peace project.

55. Spend several months learning all I can about a peace issue.
56. Start refusing when people ask me to do things that I know contribute to world conflict.
57. Do library research on a peace issue for our local group.
58. Contact a local TV or radio station and try to persuade them to give some time to a peace issue in the public interest.
59. Chair a committee in my church to decide what my congregation should do to promote peace.
60. Help write materials for a local organization (descriptive flyers, meeting announcements, calls to action, etc.).
61. Stand on a busy street corner to distribute leaflets and talk with passers-by about militarism.
62. Bring in a speaker or show a film on peace, arranging for publicity in the local media.
63. Talk with the local high school principal to find out how peace and conflict issues are covered in the curriculum, and encourage more attention to them.
64. Start a peace-oriented newsletter among people I know.
65. Attend a conference on a peace issue held in a nearby city.
66. Do in-depth research on a peace issue and write a report for a local or national organization.
67. Speak to a junior high or high school class about a peace issue.
68. Volunteer one day a week to work with a state peace group.
69. Organize a meeting to start a local chapter of a national peace organization.
70. Help organize a guerilla theatre group to dramatize issues at public events.
71. Wear a peace symbol button or lapel pin.
72. Engage in a house-to-house petition campaign for a peace issue.
73. Simplify my lifestyle as my small way of opposing what makes for global conflict problems.
74. Write an article about a peace issue for a national magazine.
75. Create a display about a peace issue and show it at a local shopping center once a week.

76. Try to persuade friends to join a social action group to which I belong.
77. Organize a letter-writing network to focus on peace action.
78. Join an organization that I know is considered radical by many community people, including my friends.
79. Write an article on peace for the local newspaper.
80. Attend a rally in the center of town protesting local government action.
81. Ask a local civic group to which I belong to have one of their meetings focus on a peace issue.
82. Talk with people at a local college or university and try to persuade them to offer a course on peace and conflict.
83. Write a will leaving some of my assets to a peace group.
84. Personally confront a board member of a corporation to explain my concern about the corporation's activities.
85. Organize a telephone lobbying network to influence my MP or MLA on peace-related legislation.
86. Stand up in a question-and-answer period following a speech and express criticism of something the speaker said.
87. Give a talk promoting peace to a local civic group.
88. Organize a vigil.
89. Serve as a contact person in my area for a peace group.
90. Give up a large portion of my leisure time to do peace-related activities.
91. Participate in a small non-violent protest, knowing that I will probably be arrested and jailed.
92. Solicit funds from local businesses to support a peace group.
93. Boycott a company that contributes to a conflict somewhere.
94. Take a job with a social action organization, even if it would mean a drop in income.
95. Speak at a local rally that is protesting government action.
96. Attend a meeting of the city council and speak to them about declaring a day for peace.
97. Travel a long distance to attend the annual conference of a national or international peace organization.

98. Participate in a panel discussion on peace given by a local group.

99. Quit my job if it is contributing to world conflict.

100. Make a speech promoting peace to a large audience at a church conference.

Now that you have completed the list, go back and find the items you marked N for "never." Try to get a sense of what makes them difficult for you. If you're in a group, do a sharing-discussion with one or two other members of the group. Afterwards, briefly write what you think makes them difficult for you – just a few words to identify the difficulty. Examples: "I find writing very difficult – I'm more of an action-oriented person"; "I enjoy talking with individuals, but talking in front of a group really scares me"; "I tend to shy away from situations where there might be conflict"; "I prefer intellectual activities and tend to avoid action groups"; "I've never had much experience at organizing and think I'd be very poor at it"; "I'm a procrastinator;" etc.

Now that you have a better idea of what things are difficult for you and why, begin to think about what you *would* like to do. Choose an item of moderate difficulty that appeals to you and that represents something you could, in fact, do now. Think through a plan for doing it, or discuss a plan with your small group. If it is something that cannot be done alone, include in your program a way of joining with others to do it.

After you have finished, write a brief description of your plan, including a time schedule for following through on it. If you are part of a group, you may want to get together with others after you complete your activity to share your experiences. You may want to talk about: (a) how easy or difficult the activity was, and why; (b) what problems arose that you hadn't foreseen; (c) what things you might want to do differently to be more effective if you repeat the activity later; and (d) your plans for the next step you want to take.

Through this exercise you are engaging in a learning and confidence-building process that you can continue at your own pace. Choose activities that will keep you moving gradually in the direction you want to go, and stay with each level until you feel fairly satisfied with your performance. Comments from others can be helpful, but remember that you are final and best judge of your own progress.

A Final Note: One thing that discourages many people unnecessarily is the feeling that they don't know enough to participate in social action. They feel that many of the actions require that one be an "expert." It is true, of course, that a few of the listed actions require some knowledge and experience, and the more you know about an issue, the more effective you can be. But one can learn in the process of doing, and most actions can be undertaken by anyone, at any stage of understanding.

Musings

Our little strength, our little wisdom is like a small candle. It is not a great light; yet, it is not insignificant. It is the gift from God that each of us has to work with. Like a small candle, it is not to be hidden under a tub, left unlit, or written off because it is not as big as the sun or the moon.

– *Bob Haverluck*

Gandhi said, "What you do may be insignificant. But it is very important that you do it." For me, a candle symbolized this attitude. It is a powerful image. It conjures up other such images in my memory, including one from my first trip to Central America.

I was in Nicaragua at the time, with a delegation of other North Americans. We were staying in a resettlement camp, where people gathered for some safety from the attacks of the U.S.-backed contras. Not a soul was in the camp who had not lost someone – mother, son, spouse, child, grandfather – to those attacks. On our last night in the camp, we gathered with a group of women to hear their stories, told with such dignity in the face of horror. We were overcome by their pain and strength. As they finished their words, the wind and clouds, which had been steadily building, swept over us all, sweeping underneath the simple roof of the building where we had gathered and drenching us.

We had planned to end the session with a prayer, asking for their forgiveness, God's forgiveness, on us. A prayer to call for healing and peace. And a simple ceremony of lighting of candles. With typical northern single-mindedness, we forged ahead, despite the wind and rain. But the candle-lighting was impossible. Each time we got a few lit, they floundered and died under the scourge of the elements. It seemed to underscore the impossibility of light in such darkness, the "foolishness" of hoping that the pin-points would be, somehow, enough.

It could have ended there. I think it might have if we gringos had been left to our own devices. We would have called it "sensible, reasonable, mature" to let the matter rest. Our hosts were more foolish, more practised in the unreasonableness of a living faith. They guided us, slowly, wordlessly, tightening the circle, closer and closer. And just as slowly, bit by bit the candles began to stay lit, just a little longer, just long enough to light another and another. Until there we were, each holding a lit candle, precarious but lit, smiles breaking, voices edging into song.

The wind died then, the rain eased and stopped, first glimmers of sun warmed and dried us, and still we sang, fools' songs, fools singing, into the sky.

– *Karen Ridd, peace activist*

Four together thinking each is alone.

A peace is of the nature of a conquest,
For then both parties nobly are subdued,
And neither party loses.

    —*Shakespeare,* Henry IV, Part 2.

The Modern Promethean attitude is one of either/or, destroy or be destroyed. It can only lead to the destruction of all in the face of the nuclear threat. Only the attitude of the Modern Job, trusting and contending within the dialogue, can lead to that confirmation of otherness which is the sole hope of humankind to avert the nuclear threat and build together a community of communities in its place.

    —*Maurice Friedman*

WORKSHOP 10

"When two or three are gathered together...": where to from here?

The strategy of these workshops has been to address peacemaking from various perspectives. We have understood scripture as integral to a proper understanding of peacemaking, deepened our ability to converse about what makes for war and what makes for peace, and experienced worship as inseparable from the activities of peacemaking. As a result, our heads, hearts, and hands are better able to respond to a violent world.

However, consumer society educates us to consume religion, ideas, and sentiments like so many products. In addition, our reticence to engage in controversy may make us hesitate to go further than merely becoming "informed about the issue." In spite of all this, some of us are beginning to find responses to peace that unite both what we think and what we feel.

This final workshop encourages us to accept the challenge of peacemaking wherever we are, with whatever tools we are given. Keeping the society and the congregation in mind, this workshop will help us to consider directions that we might take.

Objectives:
- To practice group action.
- To recall and identify individual and group insights up to this point.
- To begin with our congregational setting and to devise a group action within this setting.

PART A
(8 min.)

Activity 1
Invite folks to find a comfortable sitting position as we are about to begin a relaxation and meditation exercise. Directions should be given quietly and clearly with plenty of time between each instruction.

I invite all of you to close your eyes. Listen now to the sound of the breathing around you. Listen to the sound of your own breathing out and in, out and in. Take a deeper breath this time, and release it slowly, evenly, forcing out the last bit of breath by blowing. Repeat this – breathing in and out more deeply and slowly, holding your breath between deep breaths.

(3 min.)

Activity 2
After folks have spent a few minutes breathing slowly and deeply, tell them you are going to give them a question to ponder.

What animal or bird or creature are you on a bad day? An ordinary day? A good day?

(8 min.)

Activity 3
After a few minutes, ask people to prepare to open their eyes. On opening them, have them share their creature selves in pairs or threesomes. Ask them to identify, as much as they are comfortable, the characteristics of the creatures they've named.

(17 min.)

Activity 4
Hand out to each person a copy of the "A few words from Mr. Rat" cartoon. Before returning to their small groups, have them spend a few minutes alone with the question "What helps to make your soul like Mr. Rat? What helps to make your soul wise, like Mrs. Owl?"

Ask the whole group to make a tight circle, and then get a sampling of responses from the cartoon discussion.

(10 min.)

Activity 5
For the next exercise, you will need an enlarged photocopy or individual copies of the cartoon of the "Turtledove." This turtle, with an olive branch in its mouth and a host of faces making up its body, was originally drawn with coloured crayons to suggest the racial diversity of those faces. Because some eyes have difficulty seeing these faces, (indicated by scattered eyes, noses, and mouths), the following process is suggested:

Have group members state what they see in the picture, thereby helping one another to see it. Use the following questions to explore matters further.

- *What stories and characteristics are associated with olive branches and turtles?*

- *Is equating peacemakers with a dove-like turtle totally silly?*

(12 min.)

Activity 6
Have folks gather in groups of four to consider the following question: "How does working in groups help peacemakers?"

Workshop 10

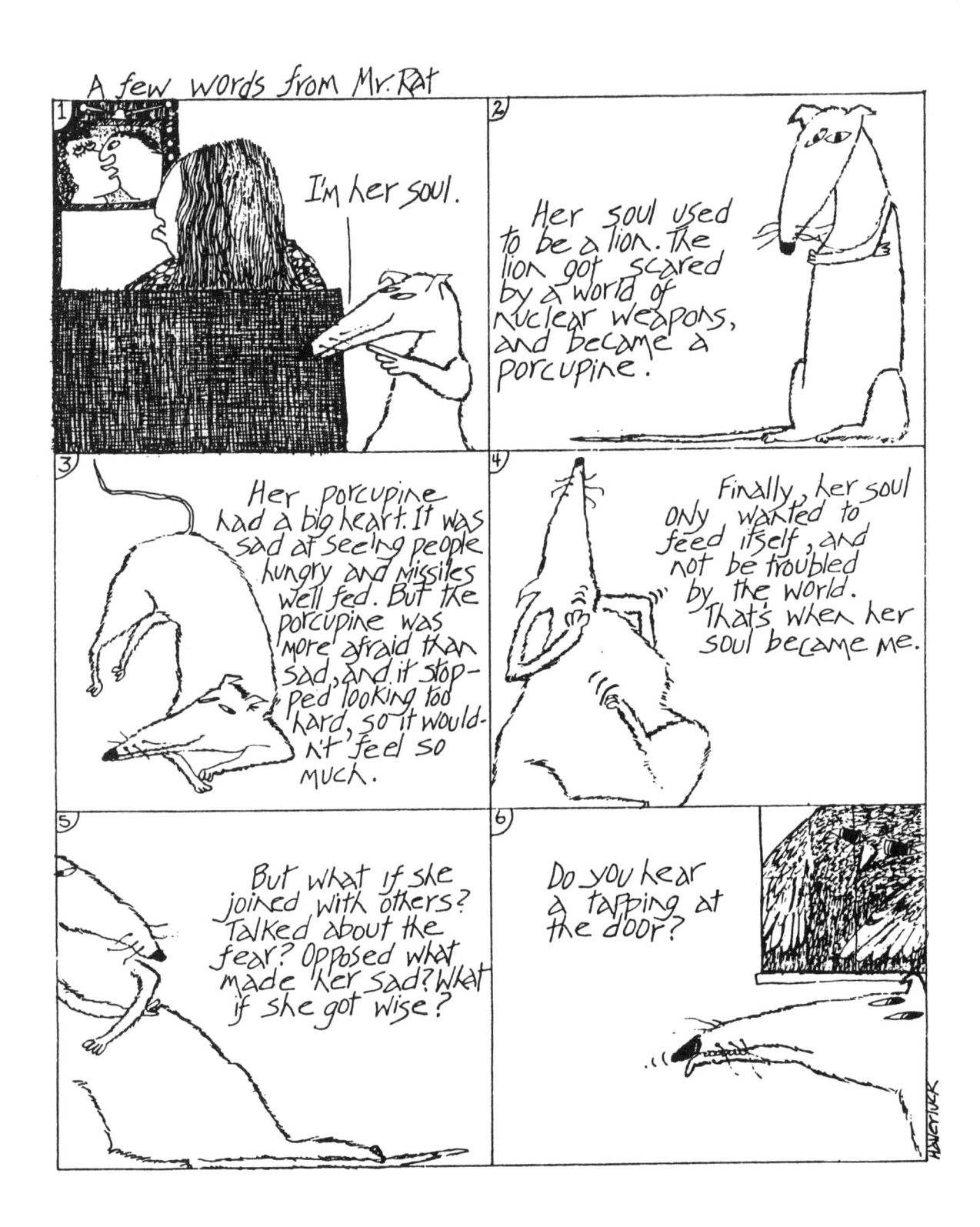

A few words from Mr. Rat

1. I'm her soul.

2. Her soul used to be a lion. The lion got scared by a world of nuclear weapons, and became a porcupine.

3. Her porcupine had a big heart. It was sad at seeing people hungry and missiles well fed. But the porcupine was more afraid than sad, and it stopped looking too hard, so it wouldn't feel so much.

4. Finally, her soul only wanted to feed itself, and not be troubled by the world. That's when her soul became me.

5. But what if she joined with others? Talked about the fear? Opposed what made her sad? What if she got wise?

6. Do you hear a tapping at the door?

Love Your Enemies

Workshop 10

(8 min.)

Activity 7
Give everyone a copy of the cartoon of the isolated individual and the seemingly immovable rock. Ask them: "What response does this cartoon give to the question being discussed?"

PART B

(30 min.)

Activity 1
Discuss the group's thoughts about possible "actions" that resulted from the past week's musings.

(60 min.)

Activity 2
The following exercise simulates a potential congregational project.

(This exercise could be the basis for organizing a peacemaking group in the congregation. In the process of meeting to develop a congregational display and worship series, key questions and positions could be explored. Our objective would be limited to getting other members of the congregation engaged in peace issues; in part by drawing upon our own discovery process. Groups may wish to complement their panels with junk sculptures, body sculptures, clowns, etc., in order to attract attention to the group. After getting everyone together once, the idea of a congregational action should be less daunting.)

In the past, I've introduced this exercise in the following manner:

I may have dreamed this. But it seems that members of the congregation have heard about your engaging of the issues surrounding peacemaking and the nuclear threat. They are very excited about this. And they would like you to create a series of large panels or displays to help the whole congregation think more carefully about these matters. The panels are to be set up in the entrance to the sanctuary. They will remain there for a number of Sundays during which time the Peacemaker themes will be developed.

The six displays will each cover a theme area which our previous workshops have engaged. I've written up six working titles to recall each area. They need not be the titles or final order chosen.

- *Images of Hope for All Creation*
- *Rethinking the Enemy*
- *Economics of Militarism*
- *The Policy of Threat and Terror*
- *Toward Security for All*
- *Following Christ the Peacemaker*

The objective here is not for you to actually create these panels, but to sketch out your ideas for what each panel might include. Draw on insights from

Love Your Enemies

...I wish I could move that rock.
I can't.
I cannot move that rock. It cannot be moved. I must accept REALITY.
That's typical! When two or three people get together— there's no sense of reality.

earlier workshops or other occasions. What might a display panel include? Images, bits of information, striking quotations, stories, poems, cartoons, drawings, photographs, key arguments, words of a song, and so on.

Ask folks to spend time alone with these topic areas, jotting down some of their own thoughts. Then they should join with two or three others to explore what might be placed on each large display panel. They should be told that they will be given about thirty minutes to work before being asked to share a key idea or two for each panel. When it is time to report to the group, consider one panel theme.

Following the exercise, ask who would be interested in working together to create such a display. Perhaps an accompanying worship service with tea and discussion following the display could be planned as well. The group would, of course, want to explore its specific options. If they managed a planning meeting before the workshops ended, they could report back to the whole group and possibly interest others in joining.

PART C

(25 min.)

Worship

This worship has an altar/table at the centre. It is decorated with a cross and one large candle to be lit at the beginning by the oldest member. On the table are different coloured candles for each participant. (The small, stubby, scented candles come in various colours and are readily available.) When you give out the candles, you'll need aluminum foil tart cups for each candle to burn and drip wax in. On the table, as well, there should be a metal or plastic washtub.

The litany, number 2, should be written up and located on a sheet of paper where everyone can see.

1. Words of Gathering:

Come you chair-riders and peace-seekers
Bring your confusion and wisdom
Bring your spirit to be set afire by God's Spirit,
The God whom we worship,
who made us for life, not death;
for mercy, not murder. Amen.

2. *Let us join in a litany that mocks our foolish sin and invites a changed direction:*

Leader: Jesus said, "You are the salt of the earth . . . you are light for the world . . . no one lights a candle and then hides it under a tub."

People: **You'll never find our light under a tub.**

Leader: What, never?

People: **No, never!**

Leader: What, never?

People: **Well, hardly ever.**

Leader: Hardly ever?

People: **All too often.**

Leader: Are we not freed to be candles of God's mercy?

People: **Freed to be small points of light in the gray confusion, in the blue despair.**

Leader and People: Small points of light signalling hope for a peaceable earth. Signalling hope to those around us, to one another, and to our own untrusting selves, God being our helper. Amen.

3. *We are going to have a reading that speaks of the Holy Spirit gathering up a crazy mix of people, the mixed multitude who gathered in the Holy City of Jerusalem and came together enthralled by the Story of the Christ. This is the story of the Pentecost, the coming of the Holy Spirit. It has nothing to do with individuals "choosing" Jesus or "taking" him as "mine."*

It has a lot to do with God's Spirit choosing all the nations, all the peoples of the earth. It has a lot to do with God's Spirit taking the language of peoples considered dirty, Godless, and dangerous – embracing it and embracing them. Just as on Mount Sinai, God's fire hallowed that noxious weed, the burning thorn bush, so the weeds of foreign nations are no longer seen to simply "babble on," but to speak in tongues that Christ is pleased to provide. The diverse ways of speaking God's love and freedom are hallowed here by a benign fiery presence.

Read Acts 2:1-13.

4. Everyone is invited to gather around the centre table and to receive a candle and a dish for the symbolic action. Then either the oldest or the youngest is asked to let their candle be lit by the candle of the whole worshipping community. Once done, they are asked to light one other person's, and that person, in turn, lights someone else's, and so on, until everyone's candle is lit.

Our little strength, our little wisdom is like a small candle. It is not a great light; yet, it is not insignificant. It is the gift from God that each of us has to work with. Like a small candle, it is not to be hidden under a tub, left unlit, or written off because it is not as big as the sun or the moon. We each have received a candle to remind us of this. Let us all hold our candles out to be lit and then return to our sitting places.

5. *In the quiet of our hearts, let us each pray to God for help to live more faithfully . . .*

Creating and redeeming God, blessed be You. Blessed be your Spirit that makes the ordinary wonderful. Wonderful are the ways you spirit the coming of your commonwealth. Your "yes" to the reconciliation of "enemies;" your "no" to the murder-suicide of nuclear warfare, are spoken in every language, in the corners and cracks of every nation. Spoken by those who know you by the name we know and those who know you by other names. Thank you for the gift of companions everywhere, whose small lights, bright or flickering, are messages of your mercy and hope. In the name of Christ, our brother and Lord. Amen.

6. Song: "With God as My Guide."

7. Benediction:

*May the Spirit of God so fill us
that we will not hunger after the ways
  that make for death.
May we so hunger for the God-
blessed healing of the nations
  that anything else will not satisfy.*

*Let us go in the blessed unrest
  of God's good company.
Amen and Amen.*

With God As My Guide

Brightly

Words and Music by Jim Strathdee

1. With God as my guide I will walk through the desert, rest by the water, run in the wind. With God by my side I will stand on the mountain, drink from the fountain of love deep within.

2. With God as my guide I will see all the talents,
   Accept the balance of who I am.
   With God by my side, say yes to the calling,
   Fear not the falling, trust in God's plan.

3. With God as my guide I will work with my sister,
   Care for my brother, bend with their pain.
   With God by our side we will rise up together,
   Strengthen each other, courage regain.

4. With God as my guide I will rise in the morning,
   Praise for the dawning beauty of day.
   With God by my side I will sing, sing forever,
   Always a lover, seeking God's way.

© Copyright 1977 by Desert Flower Music, P.O. Box 1476, Carmichael, CA 95605.
Used by permission.

Singing Psalms to the God who sets Prisoners free: an allegory

Musings

Retelling of Matthew 25:31-46

All the people of the world were gathered together. To a crowd of them, Jesus said, "You have been friends to me. You made me feel loved and so happy that I could dance and dance ten thousand years." "Wait a minute," they said. "We've heard your name and some of us speak of you in our prayers – but when have we been your friends?" Jesus answered: "When you gave food to hungry enemies; when you shared your country with people from other countries; when you visited those in prison – you visited me, you fed me, you cared for me. Like Elijah and angels, I play hide and seek with you. I hide in those made poor, made hungry, made afraid by the people who want everything for themselves. Many others shout my name on television, and wave their Bibles like clubs and whips. They roll their eyes to the sky and ignore me on the streets and in the prisons. They only make me troubled and sad. And yet, dear friends, when I play hide and seek, you find me in your brothers and sisters. And we all shine beautiful, joining hands in the opening circles of God's dancing."

Parable of the Mustard Seed

He also said, "What can we say that the kingdom is like? What parable can we find for it? It is like a mustard seed which, at the time of its sowing, is the smallest of all the seeds on earth. Yet once it is sown it grows into the biggest shrub of them all and puts out big branches so that the birds of the air can shelter in its shade."

– *Mark 4:30-32*

Genuine Dialogue and the Possibilities of Peace

"... it is just the depth of the crisis that empowers us to hope. Let us dare to grasp the situation with that great realism that surveys all the definable realities of public life, of which, indeed, public life appears to be composed, but is also aware of what is most real of all, albeit moving secretly in the depths – the latent healing and salvation in the face of impending ruin. The power of turning that radically changes the situation, never reveals itself outside of crisis. This power begins to function when one, gripped by despair, instead of allowing himself to be submerged, calls forth his primal powers and accomplishes with them the turning of his very existence. It happens in this way both in the life of the persons and in that of the race. In its depths the crisis demands naked decision; no mere fluctuation between getting worse and getting better, but a decision between the decomposition and the renewal of the tissue.

... In a genuine dialogue each of the partners, even when he stands in opposition to the other, heeds, affirms, and confirms his opponent as an existing other. Only so can conflict certainly not be eliminated from the world, but be humanly arbitrated and led towards it overcoming. To the task of initiating this conversation those are inevitably called who carry on today within each people the battle against the anti-human. Those who build the great unknown front across mankind shall make it known by speaking unreservedly with one another, not overlooking what divides them but determined to bear this division in common.

– *Martin Buber*

you're it!

Elijah the prophet playing tag

SELECTED BIBLIOGRAPHY:

Resources for the Peacemaker's Bookshelf

Austin, Richard Cartwright. *Hope for the Land: Nature in the Bible.* Atlanta: John Knox Press, 1988.

Division of Mission in Canada (of The United Church of Canada). *Moving Beyond Racism: Worship Resources and Background Materials.* Toronto: The United Church of Canada, 1987.

Fisher, Roger, and William Vry. *Getting to Yes!: Negotiating Agreement Without Giving In.* New York: Penguin Books, 1983.

Geyer, Alan. *The Idea of Disarmament: Rethinking the Unthinkable.* Elgin, Ill.: Bretheren Press, 1985.

Kovel, Joel. *Against the State of Nuclear Terror.* Boston: South End Press, 1983.

Lifton, Robert Jay, and Nicholas Humphrey. *In a Dark Time.* Cambridge, Mass.: Harvard University Press, 1984.

Melman, Seymour. *The Demilitarized Society: Disarmament & Conversion.* Montreal: Harvest House, 1988.

McSorley, Richard. *New Testament Basis of Peacemaking.* Kitchener: Herald Press, 1985.

Nelson-Pallmeyer, Jack. *War Against the Poor: Low-Intensity Conflict and Christian Faith.* Maryknoll: Orbis Books, 1989.

The Ploughshares Monitor (a quarterly newsletter of an ecumenical coalition on disarmament and development). Conrad Grebel College, Waterloo, Ontario, N2L 3G6.

Regehr, Ernie, and Simon Rosenblum, eds. *The Road to Peace.* Waterloo: Project Ploughshares, 1988.

Sharp, Gene. *The Politics of Non-Violent Action.* Boston: Porter Sargent, 1973.

Smillie, Benjamin. *Blessed Unrest: Prayers for Daily Living.* Winnipeg: Ronald P. Frye, 1985.

Soelle, Dorothy. *The Window of Vulnerability.* Minneapolis: Fortress Press, 1990.

ACKNOWLEDGE-MENTS

Grateful acknowledgement is made for permission to reprint from the following copyrighted material:

From *Against the State of Nuclear Terror* by Joel Kovel, with permission from the publisher, South End Press, 116 Saint Botolph St., Boston, MA 02115.

Illustrations from "A Tale of Two Brothers" first appeared in *The Observer*, November 1990.

Excerpts from *The Power of the Powerless* by Jurgen Moltmann. English translation copyright © 1983 by SCM Press Ltd. Reprinted by permission of HarperCollins Publishers.

From *Spirit of Gentleness*, edited by Joyce Carlson. Copyright © 1989 by the Dr. Jessie Saulteaux Resource Centre. Reprinted by permission.

From *The Politics of Nonviolent Action* by Gene Sharp. Boston, Porter Sargent Publishers, 11 Beacon Street, Boston, MA 02108. Used by permission.

Excerpts from "An Invitation to Laugh" by Bob Haverluck, *The Observer*, January, 1989. Used by permission.

Excerpt by Bob Haverluck from *Keep Awake With Me: Lenten Relections and Prayers on the Politics of God*, edited by B.G. Smillie. Copyright © 1980 by the Division of Mission in Canada, The United Church of Canada, Toronto, Ontario. Used by permission.

Excerpt from *End the Arms Race: Fund Human Needs, Proceedings of the 1986 Vancouver Centennial Peace and Disarmament Symposium*, edited by Dr. Thomas L. Perry and Dr. James G. Foulks. Copyright © 1986 by the Vancouver Centennial commission. Reprinted by permission of Gordon Soules Book Publishers Ltd.

Excerpt by William James, from the *Dorothy Day Book*, edited by Margaret Quigley and Michael Garvey. Copyright © 1982 Templegate Publishers, Springfield. Used by permission.

Excerpts from "Taking a New Look at Security" in *Ploughsharing: On Being a Part of Project Ploughshares*. Copyright © 1990 Project Ploughshares, Waterloo, Ontario. Used by permission.

From *Ammunition for Peace-Makers: Answers for Activists* by Phillips P. Moulton. Copyright © 1986 The Pilgrim Press, New York, NY. Used by permission.

"Building Confidence for Social Action" by Barry Childers. Reprinted from *Working for Peace*, edited by Neil Wollman. Copyright © Impact Publishers. Used by permission.

From "The Nuclear Threat and the Hidden Human Image" by Maurice Friedman, *Journal of Humanistic Psychology*, Vol. 24, No. 3 (Summer 1984). Used by permission of Professor Maurice Friedman.

From *Pointing the Way* by Martin Buber. Copyright © 1957, 1985 Estate of Martin Buber. Used by permission.

Peace litanies in Workshop 1 and Workshop 4 by Anne Szumigalski and Bob Haverluck.